"Michael Gehring recounts his courageous journey of faith with humor and insight. He tells it like it is and is never dull. We get the sense of a man who is confident enough of God's love and presence in his life to take a risk in deciding what to do and which way to go. Gehring is a very gifted writer and has a story worth telling."

—JEROME KODELL
Abbot of Subiaco Abbey 1989–2015

"It is rare to find a pastor-scholar who can craft a candid and self-disclosing life journal which conveys clarity and true grounding for faith and authentic conviction. Michael Gehring takes the novice lay reader and the trained theologian on a rich exploration in pursuit of living answers to challenging questions of religious integrity, the roots of loyalty, and the meaning of cultural heritage. Gehring's journey is intriguing and inviting. He respectfully invites the reader to join a development journey, filled with rich intellectual curiosity and a search in matters of the soul. He examines sensitive issues pertaining to the institutional structures of the church and their connection to personhood, relationships, and practice. This autobiographical-like story is instructive, creatively thematic, and superbly personalized. It speaks in the tone of an ordinary seeker of truth who is sharing a wealth of time-honored testimonials. Finally, it helps the reader to imagine how his or her faith choices have shaped their life destiny."

—VERGEL L. LATTIMORE, III
Ph.D., President, Professor of Pastoral Psychology & Counseling, Hood Theological Seminary

"As we travel through this life, people of the 21st century have neither the stomach nor the time for a tale of airbrushed sentimentality. With humor and humility, depth and deprecation, Michael Gehring writes his story. Rock legends and 4th century theologians are just some of his guides along the way, but it is his own voice, which speaks a truth that the world and the church need to hear. There is no pretense, no fear as he reflects on the past and speaks boldly into the future; there are only the words of one who has journeyed hard and well. Listen well."

—ROBIN CREWS WILSON
Senior Pastor, First United Methodist Church, Opelika, Alabama

As the Broken White Lines Become One

AS THE BROKEN WHITE LINES BECOME ONE

A Spiritual Travelogue

Michael J. Gehring

RESOURCE *Publications* · Eugene, Oregon

AS THE BROKEN WHITE LINES BECOME ONE
A Spiritual Travelogue

Resource Publications
An Imprint of Wipf and Stock Publishers
199 W. 8th Ave., Suite 3
Eugene, OR 97401

www.wipfandstock.com

PAPERBACK ISBN: 978-1-5326-7406-8
HARDCOVER ISBN: 978-1-5326-7407-5
EBOOK ISBN: 978-1-5326-7408-2

Manufactured in the U.S.A.   12/10/18

For my parents Leo and Mary Gehring
In the midst of brokenness,
God's love and grace
are made known.

And
In memory of
Twila Edwards, William Lane, and Hugh Kerr.
May their tribe increase.

Contents

Preface | ix

Chapter One: A Church Handed Down | 1
    I. A Band of Brothers | 1
    II. Benedictines versus Baptists | 4
    III. A Rubber Band Family | 10
    IV. Anesthesia and Amnesia | 13
    V. Olivia Newton-John and my Australian Life | 16
    VI. Barroom Memories | 18
    VII. Not Exactly Six Flags Over Texas | 24

Chapter Two: A Church Found and Vacated | 28
    I. Sort of like a John Mellencamp Song | 28
    II. Flying Spaceships and Rumors of Ma Bell as the Anti-Christ | 33
    III. Sounds of an Approaching Slow Train | 38
    IV. Bridges Crossed and Burnt | 41
    V. Ice Cubes in a Liquor Glass | 49

Chapter Three: Rebuilding the Concept of Church | 52
    I. Wondering about Lions | 52
    II. Towers Tumbling Down | 57
    III. Elmer Gantry and a Geneva Gown | 62
    IV. Three Questions | 64
    V. The Corner Crucifix | 68
    VI. Theological Transitions | 70
    VII. Homeward Bound | 73

Chapter Four: Inhabiting | 76

    I. Reichsbischof Müller, Liberation Theology, and the American Dream | 76

    II. Five-Star Churches | 82

    III. East Bound I–40, Destination Tobacco Road | 89

    IV. Churches of Excellence | 93

    V. The Lost Colony and Mexico | 96

    VI. Galloping Mustangs | 99

    VII. United or Untied: Mainline Methodism at the Crossroads | 102

Epilogue | 109

    I. Treasure Hunting | 109

Bibliography | 113

Preface

IN 1988 I GRADUATED from Princeton Theological Seminary and took my first full-time appointment as Pastor of Cavanaugh United Methodist Church in Fort Smith, Arkansas. Armed with a newly minted Master of Divinity, I readied myself for the tough theological questions. Those I couldn't answer, I felt confident an answer could be found in the truck load of books I brought from seminary. And if that didn't work, I hoped a winsome smile could see me through.

I didn't receive the questions my training prepared me for. No one got in my face demanding an explanation for the Trinity. No one even asked, "Who took out Michael Servetus?"[1] And people spent precious little time worrying about the thorny issues present in a robust soteriological account. Not a soul asked whether the penal substitution atonement theory made God into an abusive parent. They did have questions about ethics particularly as it related to sexuality. But the question I received more often than any other became the question dreaded: "Pastor, when did you convert to Christianity?"

The Oxbridge scholar C.S. Lewis converted from Atheism to Idealism to Pantheism to Theism to Christianity. Although technically speaking, he re-converted to Christianity since as a young boy he became a believer. Lewis had a significant spiritual journey through the philosophies of the age. When I explained to various individuals through the years that I didn't convert to Christianity but was raised in it, inevitably more than a few,

---

1 Michael Servetus, a sixteenth century Spanish polymath, was not only a theologian but also a physician and a cartographer. After departing from an orthodox doctrine of the Trinity, he found himself on the wrong side of the Roman Catholic authorities in France who imprisoned him. Escaping after three days in jail, he headed toward Italy but stopped first in Geneva. There he was arrested again but this time by the Protestant authorities who condemned him as a heretic and burnt him at the stake.

inquired, "But weren't you raised a Roman Catholic?" As they spoke the words, they struck my ears as if they had said that Catholics were foreigners, infidels, and unbelievers. Quizzically I would ask, "Yes, and you do know that they are also Christians?" They genuinely looked at me puzzled.

As the years went by, the question didn't go away. Not everyone who asked it thought that Roman Catholics weren't Christians, but many were still perplexed by my spiritual journey. Even though they were curious, I was not eager to describe the trip. I developed short answers to dodge the question, answers like: "Well there was this cheerleader at a rival high school, and I was a football player. . ." Another short answer, "I'm not a fan of papal infallibility. My mom always said that the Pope, just like her, put on his pants one leg at a time." As a child that answer made sense to me except that every time I saw the Pope on TV he appeared to be wearing a dress. Another quick response was, "It's Christ's table and I'm opposed to any exclusive, club-like, understanding of the Eucharist." And the last short answer which certainly raised a lot of eyebrows was, "Well technically, I never did. You know what they say, 'you can take the boy out of the Catholic Church but you can't take the church out of the boy.'"

When I joined the United Methodist Church (at Trinity United Methodist Church in Ewing, New Jersey) the pastor asked, "Michael, will you be loyal to the United Methodist Church and uphold it by your prayers, your presence, your gifts, and your service?" I resoundingly answered, "I will." I was not asked, "Do you renounce the Roman Catholic Church and all other denominational commitments, surrendering them, in order to join the United Methodist Church?"

I never resigned my membership in St. Scholastica's Catholic Church in Shoal Creek, Arkansas. Since no one asked me to, I always thought of it like possessing multiple passports. I belong not to two countries but to two denominations, though I have no doubt that some accountant personality type parish priest, with too much time on his hands, removed me from the rolls.

This account depicts how and why I drifted away from attending the Roman Catholic Church, fellowshipped for a while with the Assemblies of God (though I never joined), sojourned for a prolonged time as an outsider to the institutional church, and how I eventually found a theological home within United Methodism. What follows is an account of a spiritual journey which took a lot of turns. This work is not intended to be a complete autobiography. There is much that is not covered. I'm not going into details about my own children as I know, full well, that they would not appreciate it if I did. I am also not going into details about the courtship, engagement, and marriage to my spouse, Rhonda. Not every friendship or organization that enriched my life will be mentioned. This chronicle primarily concerns the spiritual journey that led me to United Methodism and what is was like—not only to choose it—but to also inhabit it. Frederick Buechner wrote that "the story of any one of us is in some measure the story of us all."[2] I believe this to be true and hope you will also find it so. Since this work is intended for those on various spiritual journeys, both inside and outside the church, I will provide a brief biographical sketch in the footnotes of the theologians mentioned. Also, some of the names of friends and parishioners have been changed.

I would like to express my gratitude to William Abraham, Ron Cobb, Robin Crews Wilson, Rob Fuquay, Jeff Hittenberger, Wanda McConnell, Scott Kinder-Pyle, and my siblings for reading and commenting on various drafts of this work.

---

2. Buechner, *The Sacred Journey*, 6. Frederick Buechner, the Princeton University educated writer, won the O. Henry Award and has been a finalist for both the National Book Award and the Pulitzer Prize. He has been honored by the American Academy of Arts and Letters. Buechner, described by many as one of America's most gifted writers, is an ordained Presbyterian (USA) minister.

Chapter One

A Church Handed Down

I. A BAND OF BROTHERS

IT'S ASH WEDNESDAY. I'M standing in Saint Benedict's cemetery (Subiaco, Arkansas). A Lucinda Williams song plays in my mind as I look down at Frank Stanford's tombstone, and the flat to the ground grave marker. Chiseled into it are the words "Poet" and "It wasn't a dream. It was a flood." Looking up from the ground, past the graveyard to a small pond reflecting the blue sky, then on past the brown wintered field, past the highway, my eyes fix upon the Romanesque monastery and the prep school on the hill. What Frank Stanford, I, and thousands of others have in common is that we are graduates of Subiaco Academy, a Roman Catholic Benedictine high school. We are, as advertised, a "band of brothers." Some thrived; some survived, and some are casualties lost.

Click, a picture of a grave marker is made. Due to the blinding sun, my dark sunglasses, and my seemingly dim i Phone, the composition of the picture remains hidden from me. But I'm content that the moment is captured. In some way, I've measured my mortality on Ash Wednesday. I'm a Methodist preacher on a short six-week sabbatical, and I haven't mixed, on this day, a cocktail of oil and ash. I've not chanted hundreds of times, "ashes to ashes, dust to dust." I'm a clergyman on vacation, and I'm standing here an outsider and a prisoner to and of my past. This Ash Wednesday, three vocational decades in the making, is one that will leave its mark.

"It wasn't a dream; It was a flood" is a title for a twenty-five-minute film we watched in Senior English. The teacher, a monk, Father, boxing coach (fond of his fighters and his chewing tobacco) was a legend among some, though there are others who claim that his feet were made of clay. What I liked about him is that, on occasion, when he needed tobacco for his boxers, he had no aversion about sending day students off campus to pick up nicotine for the team. I was only too happy to oblige and, for fifteen or twenty minutes, escape the bonds of that place.

From Senior English, I remember three things. One, each of us had to stand in front of the class and recite the first 14 lines from *The Canterbury Tales*. Somehow that demonstrated we were educated. But the Middle English never sounded funnier than it did coming out of the mouths with all their various accents: Saudi Arabian, Polish, Mexican, Texan, Cajun, Vietnamese, urban, suburban, and rural Arkansan. All that remains in my memory, apart from the hoot of the accents, is that the April rain broke the March drought and everyone got restless for pilgrimages. (It seems I was numbered in that tribe for marked on the front of my report card in capital letters was one word: SENIORITIS). Two, we all had to recite Hamlet's soliloquy on existence versus non-existence. And the last permanent remembrance is that Frank Stanford, who graduated thirteen years before I did, ended his life two months before the beginning of my senior year.

Father Boxing Coach said he was the most talented student he had ever taught, so talented, in fact, that he just cut Frank loose to write poetry. I wished that he had cut me loose to do anything but listen to his homespun philosophical wisdoms that dripped like Redman's from his mouth. It also would have been preferable to not endure his tales of all of the Golden Glove competitions, but watching the Mohammad Ali documentary was great: floating butterflies, stinging bees, and memories of Clay dancing feet on this Ash Wednesday.

The students could be classified in diverse ways: rich or poor, American or European, Mexican, Middle Eastern, or Southeast Asian, but the category most pronounced, in my mind and in the minds of many, was whether one was a day student or a boarder. The boarders called us "day dogs," and we, the day students, or as we referred to ourselves as "day scholars," called them "night owls." There was tension between the two groups. The day students viewed the boarders as rich, arrogant, and spoilt; the boarders viewed the day students as substandard and socially beneath them, but they also beheld them through the prism of freedom. At the end of the day, the day dogs could travel down Highway 197 to 22 and, in a few moments, have in their rear-view mirrors, not only the beautiful, European styled architectural buildings on the hill, but also the monks, the rules, and all the social trepidation. They didn't have to bear the aching loneliness that comes with being surrounded by people; the haunting forlornness which reverberates when the bell tower rings on the hour and your friends back home are gathering for a meal with their families while you're herded institution style through a cafeteria line. They, the boarders, would gladly have climbed into or on any worn down vehicle, magic carpet, or pumpkin carriage to get out of there. Yet decades later, they travel back to Subiaco, making pilgrimages of one sort of another, knowing and marking how the place and the people formed them into the men that they are.

In the second chapter of *Surprised by Joy*, C.S. Lewis told the story of his first experience in a boarding school.[1] He was nine years old, and his mother had died just a few weeks before. Dressed in uncomfortable clothes, traveling over cobblestone streets of Belfast in a horse drawn carriage, dreading the unknown, he wrestled with questions of why he and his brother, Warnie, were being sent away. Finally, they arrived at the Belfast Harbor and boarded the ship, waving goodbye to their father. They were leaving behind not only their dead mother who nurtured them, but also their home, servants, extended family, homeland, culture, city, and country; cast off like orphans so soon after tragedy had devastated their family. Traveling by train across England they eventually arrived in Watford, Hertfordshire, to attend Wynyard School. Robert Capron, an Anglican priest and headmaster, was also traveling a journey of his own which ended in Camberwell House Asylum. Lewis disdained the experience at Wynyard so much that he entitled the second chapter "Belsen" after the famed Nazi Concentration Camp.

I'm not sure that everyone who attended Subiaco felt cast off by their parents, but some did. Some wondered if their affluent parents were just too busy for them somewhat like the Lewis brothers wondered if their father's political preoccupations made them a problem that needed to be solved now that Flora had been subtracted from the equation. I remember too clearly one student, a jock of multiple sports, who was irritated

1. C.S. Lewis (1898–1963) was a tutor at Magdalen College (Oxford) and later Professor of Medieval and Renaissance Literature at Cambridge University. He is known not only for his literary criticism but also for the Narnia stories, the Space Trilogy, popular works of apologetics, and for his many other writings. For a study of his work as a lay-evangelist see Gehring, *The Oxbridge Evangelist.*

and somewhat panicked when his parents moved and didn't give him a phone number or address for an uncomfortable period of time. It was that moment that made me start to see him in a different light. To this day an image remains of him leaning on the hall phone as his fingers staccato like punched the keys calling home only to hear, over and again, that the phone had been disconnected.

Momentarily, my gaze returns to the cemetery and looking around I behold all the old German family names. They are strangely a comfort to me. Leaving, I quoted a Stanford verse;

Baby one night somebody
Going to strike a match on a tombstone
And read your name.[2]

Perhaps someone knows who he was unhappy with when he wrote those words, but rumor has it that there's no shortage of former lovers to choose from.

Walking back to the Honda Pilot, I climb in, pull out the phone and look at the pictures. Stopping at the snapshot of the grave marker almost flat to the ground, I laugh. Blinded by the sun, I took a picture with half of my shoes in it as if I'm walking into the grave.

II. Benedictines versus Baptists

Hugh Assenmacher wrote the definitive history of Subiaco Abbey and Academy.[3] On Ash Wednesday (March 6, 1878), after the mixture of oil and ash was painted on their foreheads, three monks (Father Wolfgang Schlumpf, Brother Kaspar Hildesheim and Brother Hilarin Benetz) forsook the comfort of an established monastic community and headed for the mission field. They had left St. Meinrad's Abbey which was founded in Indiana in 1854 by monks from Abbey Maria Einsiedeln in Switzerland. When Subiaco celebrated its hundredth anniversary, monks from St. Meinrad's Archabbey (the mother house) and Einsiedeln Abbey (the grandmother house) came for the celebration. We, students, imbibed the stories of how the European monks drank their American counterparts under the table.

---

2. Wiegers, ed., *What About This: Collected Poems of Frank Stanford*, 170.
3. This section is greatly indebted to Assenmacher's book *A Place Called Subiaco*.

The daring nineteenth century monks left their civilized life for the wild frontier of Logan County; not far from there, outlaws still held sway. Arkansas, at that time, looked like anything but the land of opportunity. Like much of the South, it had been economically decimated by the Civil War, taken advantage of by carpetbaggers, and limped along like a wounded faun. The monks rode in a mule pulled wagon to Fulda, then on to Troy where they boarded the SS *New Mary Hanston* traveling what was once, before the advent of the rail, the only known interstate travel way system, the rivers: down the Ohio, onto the Mississippi until finally reaching Memphis. Traveling by train to Little Rock, they rested for a few days before taking a train to the metropolis of Spadra, which remains to this day a metropolitan area that can be traversed in a blink of the eye. Crossing the river by ferry, they stepped off onto Patterson Bluff and journeyed the last leg of the trip bumping along in a wagon for fifteen miles.

If St. Meinrad's Abbey had a different abbot than Martin Marty, the monastery in Arkansas wouldn't have happened. The local bishop, who depended on the monastery for clergy to staff diocesan churches, exerted pressure on them to reduce their missionary expansion. Marty resolutely held the conviction that Benedictine DNA is rooted in mission, insisting that their work in Dakota continue. When the Little Rock Bishop, Edward Fitzgerald, and Colonel William D. Slack, Land Commissioner for the Little Rock and Fort Smith Railroad Company, cast a vision for a new monastic community in Arkansas to minister to the hoped-for flood of German immigrants, Marty agreed. Never one to be encumbered by the tiresome observance of church law, he failed to submit the new foundation for a monastic chapter vote. He wasn't the only spirited one. During the First Vatican Council (1869–1870), there were only two votes against Papal Infallibility; one of them came from the Bishop Fitzgerald of Arkansas.

The Little Rock and Fort Smith Railroad entered into an agreement with Marty that they would give 640 acres for the founding of a monastery and 100 acres for the establishment of a convent. Furthermore, they would provide $2500 to the monastic communities to aid in the construction of churches, schools, and residential buildings which meant each community would receive $1250. They would also hold 17,000 acres for a period of three years for exclusive sale to German settlers. The monastery and the railroad hired Anthony Hellmich to serve as an agent facilitating this endeavor. Marty dispatched Father Isidor Hobi. Hobi met up with Hellmich in Little Rock and together they traveled to Logan County. In December

1877, after canvassing the region, they selected the location for the new monastery which would be called St. Benedict's. They described the chosen land as fertile, flat land, ideal for farming with plenty of wood and rock for construction. Approximately twelve miles away in Shoal Creek, they found a suitable location for the new convent which would be called St. Scholastica's.[4] After Hobi returned to Indiana, he told the community that the land "is a Paradise fallen from heaven."[5]

Schlumpf, Hildesheim, and Benetz experienced it differently when their wagon, full of supplies with animals trailing behind finally arrived at the new monastic location on Ember Friday, March 15, 1878. The overgrown land had three run-down, abandoned, buildings. As the others unloaded the supplies, Hellmich and Schlumpf hiked up to the top of the ridge. Though almost dusk, enough light remained to see the countryside. Pointing to a rock formation, Hellmich exclaimed, "There's St. Peter's Chair!"[6] To this day, Academy students hike to the top of the ridge and sit in St. Peter's chair looking out over the Arkansas River Valley.

The first known mass held in Logan County occurred on St. Joseph's Day, March 19, 1878. "Known" is the operative term, for it is often told that Hernando de Soto and his soldiers and priests in the sixteenth century traveled through what is now called Logan County. The industrious monks got to work clearing the land, building the necessary buildings, and by May had built and dedicated the first St. Benedict's Church. The Indiana nuns, along with some additional monks, arrived in September 1878. In November of that same year, the nuns started a school for the children in the area of St. Benedict's. The Sisters began their residence in the new convent in Shoal Creek in January 1879 and opened another school.

In a few short years, the monks and nuns created institutions which contributed to the development of Logan County. The fledgling community established churches in Paris and Morrison's Bluff; these were in addition to the churches already established at the monastery and at the convent. All this pastoral work had to be done traveling by horseback

---

4. For the readers unfamiliar with Benedict and Scholastica, they were twins born in the fifth century in Italy. Benedict, a rich young man, lived a life of excess in Rome. After becoming disillusioned with the pleasures of the flesh, he went into the wilderness to become a hermit. In time, as his reputation for holiness grew other monks gravitated to him. He wrote *The Rule of St. Benedict* which became a standard for monastic life. His sister, Scholastica, established religious communities for women.

5. Assenmacher, 12.

6. Assenmacher, 23.

crossing dangerous creeks and streams in rain, snow, and summer heat. Quickly they established schools to teach the area children. Monks were recalled back to St. Meinrad's and Einsiedeln's, but more monks were sent. If it were not for the firm commitment of these two monasteries, it would not have survived. The Arkansas heat was miserable; the draught of 1881 unrelenting.

The monks persevered and expanded their missionary outreach starting parishes throughout Arkansas and Texas and eventually establishing monasteries in Nigeria and Belize. While doing all that, they continued to educate students through the parish schools, through the one-time Abbey College, and through the Academy. In 1891, Pope Leo XIII elevated it from a priory to an abbey and changed the name to New Subiaco Abbey.[7] The original abbey structure in Logan County burned in 1901, and a new abbey was built across the valley and up on a hill. Another devastating fire occurred in 1927, but the monks rebuilt and continued to live into their apostolate.

Driving up Highway 197 in the SUV, my mind drifts back to those days of so long ago when my brother (Tim) and I walked, in all kinds of weather, that quarter mile hill to St. Benedict's Elementary School. It seemed so much further back then. In those days, St. Benedict's, a public-school run and staffed by Benedictine nuns, belonged to the Scranton School System. Dropped off on the side of the highway, we walked up and down the hill not due to a public versus private school issue but to public school territorial demarcations.

I learned much about religious intolerance riding that school bus. Tim and I, the only Roman Catholics, were on a bus full of Protestants. The Baptists and the Church of Christ seemed the most provincial. We were told, in no uncertain terms, that we were going to burn in hell unless we accepted Jesus. I've never understood the missionary strategy of threatening the prospective convert with an eternity spent in hell. The turn or burn sermons, tracts, and evangelistic overtures seem counter-intuitive. After you've threatened someone with the cosmic sadist, then you are going to spring upon him or her that God's nature is one of radical love as revealed in the football verse (John 3:16). Evangelistic practitioners, of that kind, are giving converts the gift of cognitive dissonance. Of course, back then, we were none too intimidated by their rhetoric. We had already been

7. After Benedict fled Rome, he came to settle in a cave in a place called Subiaco. He established twelve monasteries in that area.

taught that their faith was substandard. Understanding that we were the true church, members of Christ's club, we smiled knowing that they never would be. And they, as Protesters, had a really good chance of ending up as fuel for Satan's inferno. As a child, I didn't reflect upon how close in actuality fire breathing Southern Baptists were to Roman Catholics. The irony of that passed by unnoticed.

Winding around the Performing Arts Center, I looked down at the rock wall remembering the hot July sun beating down upon us (day students) as we dug the stones out of the ground for that wall. Summers were spent mowing grass, working in the woodshop, pulling old insulation out of an attic and putting new insulation down, and countless other maintenance jobs that could be performed by unskilled teenagers. We worked until about a week before school began. It took that long to earn enough money to pay for our tuition. The monks believed in hard work and a good education and made a way for students that otherwise wouldn't be able to attend.

Pulling into the parking lot of the Coury House, I step out of my vehicle and start for the second spot of my Ash Wednesday pilgrimage. Walking past the Coury House to the rail that protects one from tumbling over the rock wall, I look out over the monks' cemetery, past the brown fields to the water of a solitary pond reflecting the blue sky. Descending the steps, I continue past the stone Chapel Columbarium to the monks' cemetery. Reading the names of former teachers who taught me art, music, and physics, I can't escape the realization, though a part of me somehow believes those years were just a short time ago, that, in reality, four decades had been spent. Reading the names of my former pastors, I took stock of my good luck and felt sorrow for those who suffered. My pastors were all, to my knowledge, good men. Their apparent greatest clergy malpractice was in the field of homiletics. Only one, in all the many years of attending St. Scholastica's Church, could preach his way out of a paper bag. For the rest, it wouldn't have taken much, a joke here or a well-timed story there, and those homiletically starved parishioners would have heralded their Father a rock star. Sometimes the priest raced through the mass; an occasion of joy for us altar servers. But then came the moment when time stood still as the priest thought reading the Bishop's inescapably dull letter a fitting substitute for the Word. No matter how they wanted to dress it up as a pastoral epistle, it was drudgery just the same.

In light of the horrific Roman Catholic sexual abuse scandal that has rocked so many dioceses both in the United States and abroad and due the media giving so much coverage to it and the excellent movie *Spotlight*, some Protestants think that every Roman Catholic altar server was sexually abused by their parish priest. Some Protestants want to believe that only the Roman Catholics are affected by this plague and that it never happens in mountain Baptist churches, in inner city congregations, in warehouse Pentecostal churches, in suburban Methodist churches, or in public schools. It's easier to believe that than to peer within their churches and schools.

As previously noted, the priests in my parish church were good men. Some had more winsome personalities than others; some worked harder than their colleagues. I never felt threatened by them, but the scandal affected the way many Catholics viewed their Church. My mother refused to give any monies which were non-designated. After the scandals made the papers, she started giving only to local parish needs, building maintenance, etc., for she did not want any of her monies going to the bishop to buy silence or to pay atonement for those "bad priests." Mom no longer trusted the Church; she was not alone.

Climbing back toward the high ground, I gazed at the stone marker for Father Wolfgang Schlumpf, the man credited as the founder of the monastery. Born in 1831, he was a native of Steinhausen, Canton Zug, Switzerland. He trained for the priesthood at the abbey school in Einsiedeln. Before coming to America, he taught classical languages and remained, even in Arkansas, a German speaker having never gained proficiency in English. These Swiss monks, for the sake of spreading the Gospel, endured the harsh Arkansas climate, the sometimes-unforgiving soil, the god-awful plague of ticks, and the suspicious Protestant neighbors. Schlumpf died three years after the fire that destroyed the monastery that he and others toiled to build.

Leaving the monks' graveyard and walking past the Coury House, I ascend the stairs into the Abbey Church. It looks like a Cathedral. Its white Botticino marble floors were imported from Italy and the rose Alicante marble from Spain. The one hundred and seventy stained glass windows were designed by a German firm, Franz Mayer Company. The altar area is dominated by a massive wooden dome and supported by eighteen feet white marble columns; suspended from it is a wooden crucifix. The dome and the cross are layered in gold leaf and the agonized body of Christ in silver. The crucifix hangs above a Botticino marble altar. Though some thought that the struggling monastery in the poor Arkansas soil and climate destined to fail, it became an orchard of life.

Dipping my finger in the cold water, making a sign of the cross, I take a seat in a pew. Listening to the silence, attending to the roar of the past, I can almost hear again Bishop Andrew McDonald, at my Confirmation in third grade, pronounce the epiclesis: "Send your Holy Spirit upon this confirmand and be his helper and guide." It's a good prayer, really. None of us, no matter how religious or not, get through this life without feeling, at times, quite lost.

III. A RUBBER BAND FAMILY

With our German last name, some of the boarders assumed that my brother and I were also from Subiaco as were a great majority of the day students. That perhaps our family, like so many of the other families in the area, had great-grandparents who bought their land from the Little Rock and Fort Smith Railroad Company. We lived a dozen miles away in New Blaine; our home church wasn't St. Benedict's but St. Scholastica's (Shoal Creek). And how we came to Arkansas from California was not due to the paternal lineage but because mom's brother, James Marion Wood, had a heart attack. Jim, a retired Army sergeant, while working in a retail business in Sacramento got bested by the Christmas rush. He headed back home to Arkansas for a lower cost of living and a slower pace of life. Mom's brothers, due to their service in the military, climbed out of the poor working white class. High school gradations weren't an option for the older siblings. Mom dropped out in the ninth grade partly to work and assist her family and partly because one day while walking home from school, a teacher stopped to give her a ride. I don't know the details of what happened, but I do remember the pain and anger in her eyes more than a half-century later as she recounted the story.

Though the Wood family was originally from Van Buren, Jim settled in Fort Smith. A couple of years later, he bought a farm house in Logan County; an area not quite as desolate as the area that the monks and nuns migrated to almost ninety years before but, in the minds of some, quite close. Grandmother took retirement from the Army Depot, left Sacramento, and headed to that land of opportunity. A few years after that, the rest migrated to the diamond state and settled in the wide-open spaces of Logan County. Uncle Jim used to say that if the Wood clan could ever pull together they could conquer the world. Like so many families tried by adversity and dysfunction, they had their fair share of wounds. Old conflicts got replayed again and again.

Mom, in a not well planned or thought out moment, left Davis, California, in her rearview mirror. Leaving in such an abrupt way, she didn't allow us to say goodbye to our father. The poor man came home and read the news in a note. She left in such an abrupt way that my sister wasn't even allowed to finish her junior year of high school even though only three weeks remained until summer break. The school counselor pleaded to let Nancy finish her junior year. Mom wasn't deterred. Her astrological sign was Taurus and she fully lived into it. Dad's sign was the same. His temper erupted and, in a moment, it was over. Mom's temper had a longer burn.

Living with the other was never easy, and the truth is they were not suited for each other even though they loved each other. This was not their first separation. A few years before that, Mom left him and they lived apart a few weeks short of a full year. My siblings thought that the divorce was set in stone but then she went back to him. Why? None of us really know, but it wasn't due to being economic dependent. He supplied the labor for the businesses, and she controlled the monies and management. This provided a great deal of frustration for him as she bought and bought. She expanded the businesses beyond his comfort level with debt. His addiction was alcohol, and hers was spending. There was, it seemed, always money for antiques and what not, but never monies enough for food or clothing. We all developed an unhealthy relationship with food.

Driving halfway across the country, leaving behind her businesses, her home, and, most especially, her husband, dragging three of her four children with her, she settled into this strange land. She, who co-owned several businesses in California, took a job as a bookkeeper for a lumber and supply company in Dardanelle. Into the middle of all her extended family members, we began our new life. Sadly, they had an inescapable pull to engage in businesses together only in the end to achieve not the elusive American dream but fragmentation. (Only Jim was astute enough to avoid that sibling trap.) My childhood memories are replete with pieces of life lying shattered and scattered on the ground; drunken uncles exploding almost every family gathering. I'd like to believe that mom had no role in the eruptions, but if I held that opinion uncontested, I would only in the end be deceived. It is painful to write these words. It is painful to come to terms with all of this. For years, I guarded it all like a well-kept secret. But my spiritual journey doesn't make sense without understanding how I idolized both of my parents and also made decisions, vows, at a very young child, to not make the same mistakes that they made. Now in middle-age, I can say that, in some ways, I have kept those childhood commitments and, in other ways, one can't ever completely outrun parental shadows.

Mom and dad's marriage was like a rubber band. They would pull and pull further and further away from each other almost to the point of breaking only to slap back together again. I spent part of my childhood wishing that they would get a divorce. The difficulty was I didn't know which parent I wanted to live with if that occurred. Dad could be frightening with his explosive temper and his drunken escapades; it was his driving while drunk that reinforced my habit of prayer. But dad could also be kind and fun.

It's amazing the tokens we keep that represent our parents. I have a couple of gambling coins from Reno, Nevada that dad forgot to cash. I've often thought I'd like to hang one of them on a chain and wear it on high holy days as I process, robed, behind the cross. It would serve to remind me that even in this life of faith there's a whole lot of chance. Never have I understood the consolation received by those who argue that in every tragedy somehow the will of God is reflected. How I've been tempted to put duct tape over the mouths of well-meaning Christians when they've said to grieving parents, "God must have needed a little angel in heaven." By their flawed logic, it would hold that God also needed six million Jews, countless number of eastern Europeans, a host of Russian orthodox priests, nuns, bishops, and a sea of people from all the tragedies, terroristic acts, and genocide of our flawed and broken world.

The choice between parents would have been a difficult one to make. Just as dad could be difficult, traumatic, and troublesome, and on other days, fun, so too the same could be said of mom. Though she didn't drink as often or as much as he did, I have plenty of memories of nights and days of her intoxicated embarrassing behaviors. Mom's emotional life could also, at times, resemble a roller-coaster. With the turbulence between mom and dad, I would have been paralyzed if the court system demanded an answer.

Vast periods of my childhood were spent believing that I didn't belong to my family. As a kid, I settled upon the consolation that some incompetent nurse in a hospital in Woodland, California, switched me, placing me in the wrong bassinet, and that my true family, normal, reliable, sober, with an above average intelligence and a winsome personality, was out there somewhere waiting for me to discover them. I spent part of my childhood looking at the TV hoping to find people who looked a lot like me. If I could just find someone who I resembled then perhaps, indeed, I would find my true, relatively normal family.

During my childhood years, when I spent a night at a friend's house, I envied that their mom cooked, nurtured, and worried about them. Never will I forget the utter amazement upon going to a friend's house and discovering that the mom kept iced tea made up all the time, so that any time you were thirsty, you could just go to that refrigerator and pour yourself a glass of refreshment: that struck me as such a luxury. In my house, there was never any shortage of beer, wine, or hard liquor to be found, but sometimes you just, as a child, had a hankering for some iced tea. That's not to say that in all the many years of serving as a bartender and waiter for dad that a little sampling didn't occur when pouring. I remember one Sunday, which was made particularly bad due to the Arkansas blue laws, that dad like dynamite detonated, "Who's been drinking all my god-damn wine?" It must have been my third-grade year or so and with intensity I prayed for God to send a fiery chariot to get me the heaven out of there; another one of the long line of unanswered prayers.

Back then if a judge had ordered me to choose, I would have chosen Grandmother.

IV. ANESTHESIA AND AMNESIA

My mother's mother was an orphan. As an adult I learned for the first time that her maiden name was spelled with an i and not a y; asking her why she had changed her name, she said, almost flippantly, "I thought it looked better that way." I wish I hadn't taken her response at face value. I wish I had probed more. Perhaps not as much as a dentist doing a root canal but, just the same, there's much I will never know because I let it lie. I also wished I had asked her why she had changed her first name from Eva to Evelyn. No doubt people do odd things but why change your first and last name, not greatly, but ever so slightly. Perhaps it was her way of distancing herself from the trauma not by looking for long lost relatives while watching TV, but by saying I'm no longer that poor little orphan girl, Eva Pearl Winn. I belong somewhere; I belong to someone. My name is Evelyn Wynn Wood.

Grandmother, born a couple of months before the beginning of the twentieth century, was only eight years old when her mother, Anis, discovered a growth under her arm. Surgery was done. Grandmother must have clung tight to her mother in those days. She never knew her father. He headed off to Oregon; his last name was never hers. As Anis's health declined, they started sleeping on the porch so her mother could breathe better. On the day after Easter, 1910, she died. For some reason, a reason lost in the passage of time, she chose not to leave her only daughter, the only testament to her life, apart from being mentioned in a census record or two, to live with relatives. (Have you ever noticed how difficult it is to find family records for relatives who never owned land, never held political office? It is especially difficult to find records for women of scarce economic means.) Perhaps they were too poor to care for Eva. Perhaps Anis feared they would put her out in the fields to work. Whatever the reason, Anis, a baptized Presbyterian, trusted the Methodists with her only child. She probably sent her to the Methodist orphanage because she knew there her child would be fed, clothed, and educated. In another place, I have written about Grandmother's trip to the orphanage by train from Van Buren to Little Rock.[8] Suffice it to say, it is difficult to imagine the grief, fear, and hope that she carried in her heart as the train rolled across the tracks leaving behind the mountainous Arkansas River Valley and surrendering to the flatlands.

Grandmother, a stabilizing force in our lives as we endured our parents' tumultuous marriage, was always there. She took Tim and me on trips. She disciplined us, cooked for us, and kept her refrigerator with treats prepared just for us. She fed us with way too many biscuits saturated in butter, covered with an ample supply of sorghum-molasses. Playing cards with us, she gave no quarter for being young. She competed at 500 with a passion, and her reprimands for boasting, on the rare occasions when we would win, were especially punctuated revealing just how much she hated to lose. She also taught us the faith.

Grandmother was pragmatic in her denominational decisions. For years she took her children to whatever church was nearest to her where they lived. It didn't matter if it were Lutheran, Presbyterian, or Methodist. When her daughter Ann went to a Roman Catholic school in Sacramento, Grandmother thought it would go better for her if she became a Catholic. For the love of her child, she gave ascent to Papal Infallibility, transubstantiation, and a male exclusive, celibate, clergy. She nodded her ascent though she never found any justification for it in the Scriptures. Grandmother knew her Bible. Joining the church so that it would go better for her daughter

8. Gehring, "Lasting Legacy," 6.

was so Grandmother; she would do whatever she could for her family, sometimes to a fault. She, who at a young age was the only one left of her family of origin, had seven children, a bunch of grandchildren, and great-grandchildren. And now as time has gone by, great-great-grandchildren.

Grandmother never knew much about her family history and, obviously, neither did the rest of us, for many years we were still spelling her maiden name with a y. It was only when my sister got interested in collecting the family history that Grandmother happened to say that she had changed the spelling of her last name.

America's great Achilles' heel, in its fascination and rush to the future, is the forgetting of its past. But it's not just the nation that forgets. The ebb and flow of time; the living and forgetting, the pain and the joys are part of every family saga. I drove up and down the highways and interstates of South Carolina for almost thirty years before I knew there was a family connection to Winnsboro. As I write this, I still haven't traveled to see the family graves of those brothers who set so much in motion. One side of me wonders, why would anyone go and take pictures of monuments to long lost ancestors? Who cares about the past that is gone? This life is busy enough. Yet, after emailing someone with an excellent Winn family tree that listed Anis and giving her Grandmother's life details, contentment overwhelmed me when I saw her, a little orphan girl, reunited with her family, taking her place in a lengthy family tradition.

Part of what has driven me on this internal exploration is what I said in the Preface: to answer the question that countless parishioners have asked giving an account of how I moved from Roman Catholicism to United Methodism. But also, part of what has motivated this exploration into family history is to retrieve what is lost. The sixteenth century metaphysical poet, John Donne, said that no one is an island. Though one is sometimes tempted to think, especially in a fit of melancholy, that one is traveling one's spiritual journey alone, such a temptation is a mirage. America's individualism and exceptionalism, long viewed by many, to be virtues, in a quick turn, can become vices that eat at the spiritual core. In this journey, I seek to explain not only my spiritual journey but the journeys of those who shaped me and to acknowledge the debts I owe.

One time, years ago, while watching Oprah, I curiously watched the Caucasians reacting defensively as others conversed about the multi-generational damage caused by slavery. Proudly patting myself on the back, I said my people had nothing to do with that. The Gehrings (of my family tree) weren't in the country at any point in the nineteenth century and the Wood family far too lowly of means. Richard the patriarch, a Baptist preacher in Sevier County, Tennessee came, according to the records, from poor but honorable people. My self-satisfactions were illusions. At the time, I knew nothing about the Winns. Now I know that they were plantation owners. What a mess it is this forgetting of history. And if I sailed down all the other tributaries of the genetic river that makes me who I am—Clyman, Joyce, O'Connor, Hampton, and York—would I find more of the same? Would I find Stonewall Jackson marching down a path only to look across the water and behold Wade Hampton III standing on the other shore?

Though it is true that Grandmother was an orphan and received no bounty, no inheritances, though it is true that Anis and her parents had no bounty to give, still one wonders about the intangibles. Now that the kaleidoscope has turned, everything looks different. Were there other non-tangibles handed down? Hold your head high—no matter how strong the storm, you will be the captain and navigate your ship—a brighter day is around the corner—You will not be overcome. Even though she lost her mother at such a tender age, did she absorb from her mother beliefs that some take for granted but are hard won for those whose ancestors were bought and sold like agricultural commodity? I'm asking questions I don't know the answers to, but I believe deep in my bones that a sense of efficacy is worth more than one's weight in gold. This forgetting of the past; it's the Achilles' heel of a nation; it's the Achilles' heel of tribes, clans, families, and individuals. It's also mine. God help me to remember.

V. Olivia Newton-John and my Australian Life

It's not just the Wood and Winn side that let the past get away. We know very little about the Gehrings and the Rosenblatts. Johannes Evangelist Gehring (grandfather) was nineteen years old when he came to this country. I've imagined the wonderment he must have felt when, finally, the endless expanse of sea gave way to the shore line. When the ship, the SS *Vaderland*, first came within view of the Statue of Liberty, what dreams and hopes did he carry in his heart? When he and his family arrived at Ellis Island, were they, like some immigrants, swindled by the workers? Human corruption remains a given. As the German-American theologian, Reinhold Niebuhr, wisely noted, original sin is the only empirically verifiable theological doctrine.[9] All one has to do is listen to the news.

After Ellis Island, Grandfather, his parents, and three of his siblings eventually made it to Northern California. Family folklore holds that Franz left Germany with his four sons and spouse, Afra, because the Kaiser had already gotten one of the sons, Ludwig, in the Prussian Army, and he wasn't going to let him have any more. They left Germany in 1910, four years before the outbreak of the First World War. I truly don't know if great-grandfather was that prescient or if it were simply a story told. Through an ad in the Catholic newspaper and with the help of two priests, John started writing letters to a woman eight years older than him, Marie Rosenblatt, a daughter of immigrants, living in Pittsburgh, PA. It is said that she could speak seven languages and picked them up working in her father's grocery store in Squirrel Hill. It strikes one as an odd way to begin a relationship, but it worked for them. They were married in Modesto in 1912.

Having heard of land grants being given in Australia, the Gehrings undertook another journey. There my father was born. There they all remained except for John and Marie. About five years later, along with their boys, they boarded a ship, the *SS Ventura*, and sailed back to California, arriving in the port of San Francisco in 1921. I've haven't found anyone yet who knows why they left Australia while the rest of the family remained there. I also have no idea why they chose to go back to California rather than Pittsburgh where her family once lived.[10]

The thought that we could have remained in Australia was a fantasy I dreamt about as a young lad. Even though I understood that truly I wouldn't exist if my father along with his family remained in Australia, still my day dreams were filled with what my Australian life might have been. Would I have one day dated Olivia Newton John? I had a crush on her in high

---

9. Reinhold Niebuhr (1892–1971) served as the Senior Pastor of Bethel Evangelical Church in Detroit, Michigan from 1915–1928. He then became Professor of Practical Theology at Union Theological Seminary in NYC. Niebuhr, popularly known now for *The Serenity Prayer*, was a Christian realist who advocated for an active engagement against the evils of Nazism and was a just-war ethicist. Niebuhr's influence is massive and crossed-over from the academy into popular culture. President John F. Kennedy was affected by his thought as well as President Barack Obama.

10. They settled in Orland and started a family business. Dad dropped out of high school completing only one year in order to help in the family business.

school. Would my closet be full of Foster's t-shirts? Would Vegemite be an everyday staple? Having heard that one needed a skill to immigrate to Australia, while in high school, I took evening welding classes at the Vo-Tech in Ozark. Unfortunately, my brother was the one with the aptitude for welding and passed all the certifications. My instructor looked dispirited every time he passed my stall glancing at my primitive artistic creations. The thought of the metal going from puddle to a perfect bead bored the snot out of me. Somehow my brother found it satisfying.

The family history of the Rosenblatts and Gehrings are lost to me. All I know is that Marie's dad was a wrestler sometime and somewhere in Europe. That he had a grocery store, as already mentioned, in Pittsburgh and died prematurely from rashly lifting a big block of cheese by himself. I haven't quite got my mind wrapped around that. And that Marie had two brothers: Leo who reportedly died at sea and Otto Martin. Taking a name from each brother she named my dad. Dad used to tell me stories about Uncle Otto. I can't remember them, but Uncle Otto's stories were funny because Dad laughed as he told them. He got that twinkle in his eyes and the burdens of the world seemed to dissipate. I've wondered if some of Dad's often repeated lines came from Uncle Otto, lines such as: "You put no more fear in me than a big ass bird." Truthfully, until I heard Dad make that comment, I hadn't thought one way or another whether it was possible or not for a bird to have a big ass.

Earlier I mentioned that my parents' marriage was like a rubber band. They would pull apart and live two thousand miles away from each other. Yet for some reason which remains a mystery to me and my siblings, they'd find themselves drawn back together again. The rest of us, having no other choice, would adjust. At a young age, we had to learn to deal with their capriciousness and with the capriciousness of life itself.

VI. Barroom Memories

It's February, and the fields look like the drought of March has come early. The brown grass is thirsty, and the workers of the fields find wetting their dryness a good way to get through the boredom of a steady array of days. Driving down Highway 197, I merge on 22 heading east toward home. Looking to my right, taking in the town of Subiaco, my how it has changed. The number of taverns decreased. One time, while conversing with a pub owner in Calver, England, he lamented the decline of the pub culture. He listed as its causes the advent of home entertainment systems, Costco's lower cost on beer and ales, and the tougher DWI laws. Similar trends, as well, have prevailed in Subiaco. My brother and I disbursed a great deal of our childhood in the bars of that village and those in the nearby towns.

My older siblings had a different childhood. Their tender years were in Davis, California and ours divided between two lands. They spent their childhood as nominal Roman Catholics, and we were immersed into Catholic culture and life. We also expended those years split between two parents. We lived for a time with Mom in Arkansas while Dad was in California. Dad's name wasn't mentioned much. It was as if Mom had just turned a page. The first year or two we lived with Grandmother until Mom bought an old abandoned rock school and so began the long process of converting it into a house.

One day a phone call came from the West Coast. The businesses were in disarray. Dad's gifts were not in management as he trusted everyone especially those who spent their evenings in the bars with him. Mercy, he loved the bars. Mom, in exasperation, one time, asked if the family should just move into one of the bars with him. That was not as funny as it sounds for a few years earlier than that they owned a bar and hotel called the Forest House. Obviously, that was a disaster. Rule of life: never let a drunk own a bar. By Jove in heaven though, he loved the bars. To this day, I remember being about four years old, in a bar in Davis, and him teaching me bathroom etiquette. He said, "Mike, these places are filthy. When you need to piss, take some toilet paper to lift the lid." Why is it with all the things I forgot from that fragile age, I remember that, an almost throwaway fragment? Of course, when Mom got the phone call, Dad had been in California on his own, unsupervised, and the businesses were about to go under. Dad's health was not good. She flew to Sacramento and put him in a truck and told him to go tend us boys, which, of course, is ironic since he couldn't very well manage himself.

Even though Dad, at first, didn't care for Arkansas, it had a good effect on him. He loved working, and he worked hard, which meant my brother and I spent our time not doing homework but stripping old wood floors of the grease and dirt that had accumulated over the decades. We also spent time clearing the land on the farm. When the sun lowered in the sky, ready for its rest, we headed to the bars. Dad made a circuit. On any given night or weekend, we didn't go to each and every one of them but certainly we hit two, three, four or more. The bars we frequented in Scranton were the

Friendly Tavern and Curly's (an apt name for a man without much hair). In Subiaco, we enjoyed many a colorful evening at the various watering hole establishments: Kennedy's, Lux's, and Triple X. In Paris, it was the Brass Rail, Fantasy Lounge, Marcel's, James' Place, the Paris Tavern, and in Carbon City, the Buck Horn. My brother and I noticed that all of these establishments had one thing in common; we were the only kids in the place, and we wondered why other kids weren't getting to enjoy the scenes. Some of the places were nice and others were rough, arm pit kind of places. We spent those years playing shuffle board and pool, eating warmed up frozen pizzas and sandwiches, beer nuts, pickled eggs, and knocking back an endless supply of soda. Dad was never stingy. People say the Greatest Generation never liked to talk about the war. That was not my experience. Sit a gregarious, inquisitive nine-year-old on a bar stool next to some stranger licking salt off his hairy wrist while chasing it down with a beer, and trust me, the stories flow. If only I had a pen and paper and the sensibility to capture it all, I could have, later, made a living as a country and western lyricist.

My favorite tavern was Steed's. Old man Kennedy made great hamburgers. Grabbing a handful of raw meat, he flattened it down with his hands and then threw it on the grill. After it cooked, he'd place it on a bun and serve it up to you, never bothering to wash his hands at any point in the process. His wife, Agnes, was kind and felt sorry for us. He prominently and proudly displayed a picture of JFK. On the wall behind the bar hung a Miller High Life clock, a Pabst Blue Ribbon sign, and next to the cash register was a shelf which had numerous brands of cigars, cigarettes, flints for one's lighter and lighter fluid. It also had aspirins, Alka-Seltzer, and Rolaids. A good number of customers bought the Rolaids after eating one of his hamburgers. But not my brother and me; we had cast iron stomachs and devoured them. Dad spent his time drinking Falstaff beer and smoking King Edward cigars.

Dad was good to us but also neglectful. One Friday evening, he dropped us off at the Academy so we could watch a football game. We must have been somewhere around the ages of nine and eleven. "Just going down to Steed's for a beer," he said, promising to return. The game was over. We waited. No sign of Dad. We waited some more. All the cars had emptied out of the parking lots; still no sign of him. The lights of the stadium started clicking off. My friend's father saw us standing there and asked if we needed a ride. "No," we insisted. "We're waiting for our father." He said, "Let me give you a ride home." Climbing in we worried that Dad would return and not find us there and, simultaneously, we suffered embarrassment that this poor man and his son had to drive twelve miles out of his way just for us and then make the return trip. We also worried about our father's safety, not knowing what happened to him. Dropping us at our home, we waited for them to drive away before we entered. Rarely did we invite someone in for we never knew what to expect. Upon seeing Dad's pickup truck parked in front of the house, we knew that one mystery was solved. When we went inside, the house was dark. My brother and I, talking and stumbling around, jumped when a light suddenly came on. Dad stood there stark naked pointing a loaded pistol at us. He thought we were robbers. The man got so drunk that he forgot that his children were at the ball game and came home and went to bed. All he said before turning to go sleep it off was, "You damn kids, quit making so much noise." Really, that's all you've got to say? I thought, "Sorry that I abandoned you" would have been a better start. Of course, with Dad, one waited, in vain, for an apology.

Some years back I wrote an article about the emotional struggles some experience when the cultural celebration of Father's Day rolls around.[11] Writing the article was easier than deciding whether to publish it or not. That was agonizing. As a child of an alcoholic ingrained in me were the words, "Don't talk, don't trust, and don't feel." There is a certain numbness that comes with all of that. My Mom's number one family system rule was to deny it. When I got into my high school years, I referred to Dad as an alcoholic. By that point, he had already been dead some years. Every time I did, Mom got upset and corrected me: "Your father was not an alcoholic; he just sometimes drank too much." "Yes indeed," I replied. "He drank too much seven days a week and fifty-two weeks a year." Mom didn't understand that not only was I angry at my father for all the pain that his alcoholism caused but also that I sought to understand it as an addiction. By naming it as a disease, I struggled to redefine it so that I could move past the anger and reach for compassion.

Mom also had trouble understanding that I held her accountable, as well, for her negligence. She portrayed herself as a victim to Dad's weaknesses but having lived with both of them without the other one present was a great clarifying tool. Mom played an active role in the drama of our family dysfunction. Sometimes it was overt and sometimes just plain odd. An example of the odd is when she took us to the Sacramento airport. This was in the old days when security was loose and one could wait at the gate

11. Gehring, "Choosing to forgive Dad," 6a.

with those traveling. Back then they had machines in the airport where you could buy a life insurance policy on yourself or a fellow traveler. My brother and I stared in disbelief as she fed her dollars in the machine purchasing a policy on each one of us. She then hugged, cried, and sent us through the door to board the plane. She left the airport with the policies in her purse as we found our seats on the plane. Looking at each other, we wondered if she knew something that we didn't. Was she hoping that the plane would crash and we would die? Who knows but she certainly hedged her bets. We were children traveling without airport chaperones. You had to pay extra for that. As we navigated changing planes and terminals in the Dallas/Fort Worth Airport, we did so without any significant monies in our pocket. Cell phones hadn't been invented. All we knew is that we had to catch that plane and so we did. My childhood is replete with stories like this; I just don't have room to tell them all. And, even if I had space enough, I don't want to write them in stone.

The virtue of raising your children this way is that early on a sense of self-sufficiency is bred. Later, Mom regretted that independent streak in us. When I reminded her of these events, after decades had passed, she had difficulty seeing herself as neglectful. Many conversations were spent on these childhood years. Though I can't say we ever totally agreed with the other about her role in it, I can say we got better listening to the other. And that process of listening was a balm for our souls.

Dad died when I was eleven, and I greatly missed him. When it was just the three of us living together (dad, my brother, and myself), there were no knock down family fights. When not working on the farm or at the house or when we were not in the bars, we would sit around and watch TV together. I have a vivid memory of Dad telling me, when I must have been about 9, that if I ever got a girl pregnant, he would hire the best lawyers in the country and prove that I was not the father. I appreciated the sentiment, but the difficulty resided in that, at the time, I didn't know how girls got pregnant. I remember watching Hogan's Heroes together and him laughing and then saying, "Now Mike, just remember it's all fiction. It wasn't really like that." I also recall watching the news together in the early 1970s with all the rhetoric about the evil empire of the Soviets, and Dad saying, "Mike, those Russian people are good people. It's their government that's bad." Then he told me how Russian doctors had saved his life during the Second World War. Grandfather Franz saved his sons from the Kaiser, but Uncle Sam got his grandsons and great-grandsons.

I love both of my parents, but it's only fair to say that if any social workers had been roaming the lands where we lived, they probably would have taken us out of the home. Often there was not enough food or clothing. I remember one time I won a contest in school for reading the most books and earned a trip to go to Booneville (a place I had never been before) to an event with other kids who had also won their reading contests. I had taken to Grandmother the only pair of pants I had that didn't have holes in the knees. It had a rip in the crotch but she mended it. That morning as we waited for the bus, my brother and I wrestled and the fixed seam ripped open. Having no other choice, I put on a pair of pants that had both knees ripped open. When I got to school, Sister H shamed me in front of the class. Her words still echo in my mind as she wondered out loud, in great agony, what possibly could I have been thinking and that I wasn't fit to represent St. Benedict's. She appointed someone else to go in my stead. He hadn't read as many books as I had, but his pants also didn't have knees protruding through them.

It is true that my parents didn't take care of us as they should have. Yet I also want to say that my parents were more than their weaknesses; they were more than their brokenness. Mom died when she was eighty-eight. By that point, Dad had been dead for forty-two years. Since his death, she had dated a good number of men and even married again though that was short-lived. There weren't many men who could handle her ways. Because I lived in North Carolina, for the past few decades and she in Arkansas, we normally saw each other once or twice a year for a week or two at a time. But we talked on the phone two or three times a week. In one of those phone conversations she amazed me. She said she had been reading, over and over again, Dad's letters to her. She said that he was the only man that she ever truly loved. That surprised me as I did not know that she had even kept his old letters.

It's Saturday, March 1973, two days before Dad died. My brother and I were watching TV when Dad came into the living room, showered, dressed in church clothes, wearing Old Spice, announcing that he was going to church. We looked as if we had been struck dumb because he never went to church alone and, rarely, did he go with us. On the way into the sanctuary, he passed Sister Teresa, one of the two nuns stationed at St. Scholastica's (Shoal Creek) to look after the old convent. It was just a shell of its former glory; the main mother house is now in Fort Smith. Sister Teresa, a heavy-set woman with a round face who by no means was a pushover, had a kind heart. As he drew near to her, he placed his hand on her shoulder and said, "You remind me of my mother." After he died, she shared with us that story believing because of the way he spoke to her, due to the way he was present to her, that he had a premonition he was going to die. Of that I know very little but what I do know is that evening, before going to mass, he did something quite atypical. My father was never one for apologies. He and my sister had gotten crossways with each other a week prior. Before leaving for mass, he called for her to come out from the kitchen and he hugged her. It was a silent apology.

VII. Not Exactly Six Flags Over Texas

Early in 1974, Mom needed to go back to California. This was not unusual as she made many trips back and forth looking after Davis Van & Storage. What was different this time was that Grandmother wasn't there to look after us. She was in Arizona. Dad was dead. My sister was married, and my older brother, in faraway lands, pursued a military career. No one was left to look after us. When Mom broke the news of her trip to the West Coast, she mentioned that we would be staying with Sister Teresa and Sister Coletta at St. Scholastica's Convent.

My brother and I asked, "What do you mean? They're not family. They're nuns. What do they know about kids?" Always the optimist, she, as she glad-handled our experience of life's unpredictability, said, "Oh, you all will have such a good time with the Sisters. And you all will have great fun feeding the cows." We didn't buy that for a minute as we had cows of our own and feeding them was no *Six Flags over Texas* experience. Though my brother and I protested for a few moments, Mom insisted and we, being children without options, relented.

She flew away and we were grounded in a nunnery. I wish I could tell you it was absolutely awful. I would like to draw a portrait of some Dickensian orphanage but the truth is, they took great care of us. They cooked three meals a day on weekends and two meals on school days. Lunch ordinarily at St. Benedict's elementary school, institutional fare, was welcomed but now we longed for the Sisters' cuisine. They cooked real food, not some Morton's frozen pot pie that you were lucky to find hidden under a bag of ice. Though I will tell you there was such a scarcity of staples in my house that if you found a frozen pot pie, you felt like exclaiming "Eureka," as if you had just won the lottery, but you didn't dare; just as those miners in the

California gold rush wouldn't have exuberantly yelled for fear that someone would stake a claim. The nuns made sure we did our homework and they doted on us. Tim, being two years older, got to drive Sister Teresa's jeep. She wouldn't let the nuns from Fort Smith drive her jeep when they came to slum in the wilderness. She didn't have much use for those who refused to wear the traditional nun's habit.

My brother and I lived in the huge guest house and only occasionally had to share it with church groups or couples doing retreats. Sadly, the building is no longer there. The Sisters lived in what was once the old infirmary, one of the few buildings not burned down to the ground when a nun, in 1940, let a brush fire get out of control. After dinner and homework, we would sit around the table and play 500. I swear Sister Teresa changed the rules as the game wore on. Like Grandmother, she intended to win. They lectured us about being good sports, but Sister Teresa got cantankerous when she lost. Sometimes Father Columban would come for dinner and sit in on a hand. He, the parish priest, was also Subiaco Academy's librarian. Possessing an inflexible rule that yo-yos were not allowed in the library, he confiscated them from the offenders letting them know that they had forfeited all ownership rights. This was a bonanza for my brother and me as he gave us all the contraband yo-yos. I don't know how long we lived with the nuns but my sister estimated that it was for two months until Grandmother returned from Arizona.

Before and after our stay with them, those nuns were a fixture in our lives. Ours was a small parish, and there were not many altar servers. At Christmas, they gave us holy cards, medals, candy and a gift of some kind. At Easter, we got candies of various kinds and a huge Pascal lamb made out of Rice Krispies and marshmallows mixed together. It tasted so good but disappeared like manna in the wilderness. Those nuns took care of that parish making sure there were fresh flowers on the altars and showering concern on the parishioners. Sister Teresa and Sister Coletta hoped beyond hope that Mother Superior would leave them alone and let them die in Shoal Creek. It was not to be; a decision came down from Fort Smith. Jesus said to Peter that one day someone will bind your hands and take you someplace that you don't want to go. It happened to them. Tears rolled down their wrinkled faces when the news was delivered and even more flowed when Shoal Creek grew fainter in the rear-view mirrors.

Exiting Highway 22, turning left onto the Old Military Road, I cross over Pee Dee Creek and gradually climb the small hill. Passing the convent, memories rush by. There to my right is the old cemetery for the first nuns of the convent. It looks so small to me now but as a child I thought it was as big as Arlington. It probably should have only taken me thirty minutes to mow and weedeat it but, with all the in between times of crying old loud lamentations to God, it probably took more like two hours. Everything seems magnified in childhood, and it is true that sometimes children have no options but to ride out the storms which blow their way. But with all the turbulence, unpredictability, the family turmoil—still with all of that—there were these two nuns who bore witness to God's grace.

Some months ago, while traveling with my brother to Ozark, I asked him, "Why do you think we made it through our childhood without ending up in prison?" He quickly listed without even thinking about it: Grandmother, Uncle Jim, Sister Teresa, Sister Coletta, and Father Columban. I agreed and, though it may surprise you, I added Sister H to the list. Yes, she shamed me in front of the class, but I also knew that she always wanted the best for me. She just didn't know how to help. It was Father Columban's dream that I would become a priest. He seemed puzzled when God led me down a different path.

As I look back at my childhood all these decades later, I realize now what I didn't understand then: the power of osmosis. Benedictines take three vows: the vow of obedience, the vow of stability, and the vow of conversion of manners (life). These are vows not made in one's own private quarters. They are public professions made in front of the community and in front of all of the guests at the service. These votarists are counter-cultural and gave me an insight into a spirituality that I probably would not have gotten in the United Methodist Church. They didn't spend their time attempting to court and prove their relevance to a contemporary culture. They didn't find themselves in a post-Christian liberal theology faith crisis. They were more communists than the Marxists though I doubt Sister Teresa or Coletta had ever read *The Communist Manifesto*. I and a couple of friends, as undergraduates, read it out loud on a road trip to Mizzou, and I pondered how the sisters lived such incredibly full lives without ever owning anything. They were free from so many of the prisons in which we confine ourselves. Ownership, amassing wealth, though not intrinsically evil, are great temptations. They can be illusions, whereby one deceives oneself into thinking that one can insulate oneself from life's capriciousness and dangers. In the end, as life moves on, as possessions, power, and control are stripped away, all one has left is God. All one has left is God as one passes through the neck of the hour glass moving from the community of friends and family of this world to the community of the Church Triumphant.

I grew up with stories. They told me the story of St. Benedict making the sign of the cross over a chalice filled with poisoned wine and a snake rising up out of the liquid. It seems that the monks of his community thought him too tough of a task-master and decided the easiest solution was to kill him. They told me about a misbehaving altar boy who doubted transubstantiation. Stealing a consecrated host from church, he took it home. In his room, taking out a straight pin, he stabbed it, and the blood flowed. These nuns were not modernists; they were robust supernaturalists, and they wanted to make sure that I was properly cautioned. They loved to tell the story of how Benedict, impatient, needing to get back to work, wanted to depart from visiting his sister. She prayed for a longer stay, and God sent a storm forcing him to remain through the night. As they told the story, their eyes sparkled. As a child, I never understood the sacrifice they made for an institution which treated them like second-class citizens. Just because of their gender, they would not be able to preside over the Eucharist. No wonder they loved to tell the story of God hearing the prayer of the woman.

My childhood taught me not to expect life to bend my way but it also, in unexpected ways, gave me significant spiritual resources for the journey.

Chapter Two

A Church Found and Vacated

I. Sort of like a John Mellencamp Song

ONE DAY WHILE CROSSING the Ada Mills Bridge that spans the Arkansas River, I wondered why my brother and I didn't spend our high school years cruising Clarksville. We certainly needed a diversion from the monotony of continuously circling the Paris Court House in our 1976 Blue Datsun pickup truck. Paris, a town of fewer than four thousand, did not offer many opportunities for teenage entertainment. In Clarksville, other hang-outs abounded as well as another courthouse. Why didn't we partake of the nights of Clarksville? Confining ourselves to the Pizza Barn, we spent an untold number of quarters playing pinball or video games. If only we had been savvy enough to buy stock in a little retail chain that recently opened a store in Paris: Wal-Mart. But we were too busy indulging in the all-you-can-eat-pizza buffets to ever fashion ourselves a Warren Buffet. Later that same day, I asked my brother, "Why didn't we hang out in Clarksville?" He responded, "Duh, the bridge wasn't opened then." "Oh," I answered, "that makes sense." Most people don't cross bridges that aren't there, at least, literally speaking; figuratively, people do it all the time.

Looking back over the many decades, without even realizing it, I crossed bridges which led me from Roman Catholicism to Protestantism. As a child, I was deeply immersed. While riding my banana seat bicycle weaving in between the broken white lines of Highway 22, I sang not a Beatles tune, but belted Sister Janet Mead's 1973 hit, *The Lord's Prayer*,

28

which was burning up Billboard's Top 100 in 1974. In those years, I prayed regularly despite all the silence and the non-answers. Not only did I faithfully wear my green scapula but, in addition, on the chain around my neck hung a Benedictine cross and a medal of one saint or another. With a brass chalice, a gift from my sister, I celebrated mass for my invisible friends and parishioners. In second or third grade, I started feeling a call to the priesthood. Burned into my mind, in those days, was the line from the mass about Melchizedek. I didn't know who he was. I didn't know if he had been an apostle, bishop, or local clergy. I didn't know where or when he walked on the earth. I didn't even know if one found him in the Old Testament, the New Testament, or in both. All I knew is that at a very young age I felt called to be a priest in the order of some dude I didn't know.

After graduating from eighth grade at St. Benedict's, I crossed the street to attend Subiaco Academy. Subiaco required its graduates to take two years of foreign language so during my junior and senior years I took Spanish with Father Eugene. He was a bit of a mystic who recorded his dreams. Taking a page from him, I started doing the same. As time went by, I mustered the courage to share my dreams, and he did his best to interpret them. During my senior year of high school, from time to time, I also attended a charismatic mass, which was very different from the staid Roman Catholicism of Shoal Creek.

The cliché from Hollywood movies and from everyday life is so true: it's never just one thing. It's not just one event, one bridge that leads you into a new direction in life. It may seem that way and for many years when asked why I left Roman Catholicism for Protestantism, I answered, "Loretta." Beginning the down-home yarn, I said, "She was a cheerleader at a rival high school, and I was a football player." The parishioner's mind would drift in the direction of romance. Truth is it wasn't just Loretta that captivated my attention. It was also her whole family. Her mother and father were devout. The entire family went to Midway Assemblies of God Church, and I started attending with them. Her mom cooked for the family and also nurtured them. She did the same for me even after Loretta and I broke up. The romance was over, but still there I was watching TV, breaking bread, or just talking about life. I'm sure her new boyfriends found that perplexing. Her father was steady and sober never prone to volcanic eruptions. Every family has its own challenges, for sure, but I'm only describing that which I knew. Every day didn't bring a new crisis. Every day the pendulum didn't swing from financial gain to ruin. They were reliable. You knew what to expect when you opened the screen door entering their house. I don't want to turn them into plastic saints but, compared to the chaos I called home, it seemed a step in the right direction.

Mom didn't understand why I spent so much time at their home and, at that age, it was not easy for me to explain. But that home was a balm for my soul. During that time period, I started reflecting critically on my church. Part of it was due to their influence and part of it stemmed from my catechism classes. As I thought about grace and judgment, my soul became troubled by the inconsistencies of Roman Catholic teaching and practice and by my father's exclusion from the Eucharist. What disturbed me greatly, what angered me, was that my father needed the grace that the sacrament provided, but the institutional church banned him from that means of grace. As already mentioned, my father was married and divorced long before he met my mother. He had a child from that marriage. As a divorced Catholic, the only way for him to receive communion was to get an annulment. An annulment would declare his first marriage invalid and, in his mind, would also state that his daughter from that marriage was illegitimate. He loved her, and he refused to make her a bastard.

Now the great scandal of all of this was two-fold: first, I knew a parishioner in my home church—it was a small community—who not only received communion with his wife but also with his lover. I also knew that the priest, who was dispensing the wafer, knew about what was going on in those relationships. And of course, that parishioner, a very affluent man, strongly supported the parish. And second, I also heard of priests who had affairs and who were still presiding over the Eucharist. And now, all these decades later, after the movie *Spotlight* came out, we also know that archbishops, bishops, and others in the hierarchy deliberately moved priests who had molested countless numbers of children to new parishes. The institutional church, which allowed child-abusing priests to continue to celebrate the Eucharist, walled off the Eucharist from my father. My father who wouldn't deny his own daughter was denied the sacrament. This indignation over my father's treatment burned in my soul. It burned like an inextinguishable inferno. The church, called to be an agent of grace, became, for me, an institution of exclusion, oppression, and contradictions.

During my senior year, I continued attending mass at St. Scholastica's and Subiaco, and I also visited Midway AG. I heard some priests say that Protestants had an inferior faith and others, who were old school, told me that Protestants were children of rebellion and destined for hell. Subiaco had its fair share of old guard Catholics. One priest disclosed that the saddest day of his life occurred when he had to turn around and face his parishioners. Obviously, he was not a fan of Vatican II.

My girlfriend's church possessed a seemingly simple message: just believe in Jesus and experience the power of the Holy Spirit. I loved that. No one was excluded from communion; it didn't matter if you were divorced, single, or married. They passed the tray around and you could help yourself. They didn't say that, in order to partake of the elements, one had to agree with all the core teachings of the Assemblies of God. They just said, "Grab and partake; be healed." As a child of an alcoholic, I found their worship emotionally liberating. For too long I had been taught not to trust emotion and here were people who let it all out: lifting their hands, being slain in the spirit, speaking in unknown tongues, and dancing around in joy. Some of those women could really dance.

Of course, it wasn't paradise. I didn't agree with everyone and everything that I heard. One day after a service, an elderly man attempted to cast me into a prefabricated form. I resisted such efforts. The background to the story is that during my senior year, Mom decided to open the Trading Post Mini Mall in our old home. After building a home on the farm, she converted the old school into a convenience store where she sold groceries, fishing licenses, and antiques. It quickly became the meeting place for the community. Tim and I were relieved that Mom now had other people to talk to besides us. In a small community like ours, widows often were treated like third wheels at best and at worse potential hazards to social stability. Mom needed something to keep her busy. Everything changed dramatically after she applied for and received a beer license. All the surrounding counties were dry and the business took off. I still find it odd that she chose to trade in the commodity that caused our family so much grief. The store was now no longer her solo pet project, but we got drawn into it. Reflecting on the irony of all that as I wheeled out cases upon cases of Old Milwaukee, loading them in the back of some cowboy's pickup truck, as my eyes fell on impoverished children in the cab. I'm not a teetotaler. I enjoy a good glass of merlot as much as the next Methodist preacher, but her choice struck me as perplexing, just as I found it strange that many of our family Thanksgivings and Christmases were crashed by drunks we didn't know who she invited because she felt sorry for them.

Standing in Midway Assemblies of God Church after the service, someone introduced me to this elderly couple stating that I'm from New

Blaine. The old man said, "You all made a big mistake." I replied, "How so?" He said, "By letting beer into there." Not realizing that the woman who had got the license was my mother, someone quickly whispered in his ear. He turned beet red. In my family system, we get frustrated with each other, but we close ranks to outsiders. Firmly, I said, "The real mistake was from all those supposed and ever-so-superficial Christians who protested the state's decision by dumping trash bags full of empty beer cans in our front yard." I still remember the ire I felt from their supposed Christian witness, especially since I was the one who had to pick up all those blasted beer cans. As he retreated, I wanted to sing, "Oh what a fellowship. . ." Being a part of the church is not for the faint-hearted.

Leaving Rome was like slipping out the back door. It was not really as much of a departure as it was a drifting away. There was no sudden break. No defiant denunciation. No 95 theses nailed to a church door. I carried a picture of my father in my heart, an exile from the Lord's Table, banished from the sacrament and I just wandered away. Carrying him with me, I went off in search of a better way. I never joined an Assemblies of God church, and, even with all my hard feelings about how my father was treated, never withdrew my membership from St. Scholastica's Catholic Church. I felt led to go on a pilgrimage to some destination that I didn't know. And for some reason which escapes me and seems illogical to me, I just trusted that God would go with me and it would all turn out alright. To this day, I can't explain why I possessed that deep and abiding faith in God, especially in light of the chaos, abandonment, hunger, violence, and despair of my childhood. Perhaps, somehow, as a child, experience hard-wired into my brain this realization: when all have failed and disappointed, when you've looked every place and found no consolation, still hanging around your neck is that testimonial, that crucifix, that witness that God co-suffers with you. Back then when I believed that somehow it would all turn out good, I meant that it would all turn out okay in this world. Rattling around in my brain was Romans 8:28: "We know that all things work together for good for those who love God, who are called according to his purpose." (NRSV) What I didn't understand, all those decades ago, but feel deeply now is that some things, some injustices, will only be made right in the kingdom of God.

II. Flying Spaceships and Rumors of Ma Bell
as the Anti-Christ

Though it is accurate to say that I never joined the Assemblies of God, what that statement does not reveal is just how deep into the water I swam. The majority of my friends were "Jesus-freaks" and some classified me in that group as well. There's a picture of me standing in front of a Miller's Beer truck wearing a Smokey the Bear t-shirt pointing to heaven and saying, "Only He can prevent eternal fire." During my freshman year at Arkansas Tech University, I attempted to proselytize my fellow hall mates in a dorm that reeked of marijuana, stale beer, and vomit. Mass attendance greatly lessened that year. I was a regular at First Assemblies of God Church in Russellville and endured some fairly strange sermons. Jimmy Carter was president; the Iran hostage rescue mission had failed and apocalyptic fever was in the air. People were sure that Jesus was about to split open the skies and some people were going to disappear while others endured hell on earth. Of course, all this depended on whether you were pre-tribulation, mid-trib, or post-trib. These experiences reinforced the belief that the city of religious tranquility was not to be found on this side of eternity. One guest evangelist preached that Ma Bell was the Anti-Christ. This sleuth of an evangelist discovered this epiphany when the telephone repair man fixed his home phone. The repairman said that there were three blue wires in the phone each numbered six. One can imagine the phone man laughing his ass off as he drove away. Obviously, the evangelist was no Father Brown. We also learned from another preacher that the Anti-Christ was, in reality, a computer in Brussels, Belgium. Now all these decades later living under the tyranny of the automated age, I confess he may have been on to something.

The protagonist in Walker Percy's novel *The Thanatos Syndrome*, Tom More, discovered that his town, Feliciana, had its water supply contaminated with heavy sodium resulting in some fairly outrageous behavior. I've long been convinced that some kind of heavy religious element exists in Arkansas' water supply. What else can account for its steady production of religious zealots? One time my brother, an avid collector of antique cars which litter our farm, was in a junk yard seeking old car parts. Tim and the old man who owned the salvage yard got into a conversation. Before long, sensing my brother's goodness, the salvage yard owner decided to reveal that God told him the world was nearing its imminent end and that he was to build a spaceship to flee the planet. So out of aluminum and other various metals, this modern space day Noah constructed a spacecraft to flee the planet. It looked like one from the cartoon *The Jetsons*. My brother said it was even complete with a chair that when you cranked its side lever, it elevated into a glass bubble. It's important when one is engaged in interstellar travel to be able to see the asteroids so you can out maneuver them. The man gave Tim a complete tour of it except for the engine. He said that NASA engineers had traveled to his junk yard demanding to see it, but God told him not to disclose the engine's secrets. Can you imagine how incredibly disappointed they were as they drove empty handed the many miles back to headquarters?

Though I love my home state as much as the next Arkansan (we are all a bit rabid about it) yet it's only fair to warn outsiders about the heavy religious element. It wouldn't be right for some hard-core secular New Yorker to only be passing through I-40 on his or her way to California to pitch a TV pilot and all of a sudden start having visions of Jesus. When traveling through Arkansas, you might only want to drink water bottled out of state. I promise you it's worth the few extra seconds to check the label.

There was another man who was sure that God told him that the world was about to end. Reasoning that he wanted to be as close to Jesus, as possible, when he divides the skies and descends, he moved up on top of his roof. The man waited and waited. Sadly, Jesus didn't come for him, but the Sheriff did as the man had stopped making payments leaving the bank to repossess. When it's a power struggle between God and mammon, isn't it ironic how many times mammon wins. The man had no doubt whatsoever about the genuineness of his religious enlightenment. A revelation broke into his consciousness like a lightning bolt, and he possessed no criterion to help him sort through it.

There are so many stories like these that one would grow weary collecting them all. Sometimes it seems like almost everyone has had a heavenly visitation of some kind or another whether angel sightings, or a tuxedo-wearing hitchhiker who disappears after telling the driver about Jesus. Stories abound of visions, dreams, near-death experiences, and prophecies. Arkansas produces rice, country western musicians, politicians who sound like preachers, and no small number of religious enthusiasts and fanatics. So, it shouldn't surprise anyone that in 1914, in a town famous for its healing waters, bars, illegal gambling, horse-racing, and prostitution that a major Pentecostal denomination was founded. Hot Springs is also, by the way, the home of Bill Clinton where he spent his elementary through high school years.[1]

To understand why some felt the need to systematize the fire of the Holy Spirit, it is helpful to remember the early history of the Pentecostal movement. Often Pentecostal historians begin the story of the birth of the movement with Charles Parham. Parham started preaching at the age of fifteen. He attended a Methodist institution of higher learning, Southwestern College in Winfield, Kansas. Eventually feeling that the Methodist Church was too constraining, he left it and founded the Apostolic Faith Church. In 1900 in Topeka, he also founded Bethel Bible College. And like many fundamentalists and fanatics through the ages, he was, proudly, a man of one book. The forty or so students who attended Bethel Bible College got a real break on the textbook bill. The Achilles' heel of the Pentecostalism, for many decades, was its fear of higher education. Young Pentecostals were often warned against going to secular universities with the dire prophecy that if they did, they would lose their faith; perhaps gaining the world, but forfeiting their souls. Parham taught the students to seek the fullness of the Holy Spirit and instructed them to fast and pray while he was away preaching a revival. On January 1, 1901, a student began speaking in tongues. Parham identified speaking in tongues as the initial physical evidence of baptism in the Holy Spirit which is a secondary experience to salvation. News of the out-pouring of the Holy Spirit spread far and wide and others came seeking the gift of glossolalia. Bethel Bible College was only open for about two years, but Parham continued preaching and teaching his message to a wider audience.

One of those who heard Parham lecture about the Spirit's empowerment was an African-American preacher named William Seymour. Seymour, born in Louisiana and baptized a Roman Catholic, moved in his twenties to Indianapolis and became a born-again Christian in the Methodist Episcopal Church. In his thirties, he was in Texas attending Charles Parham's lectures. Seymour, the son of former slaves, had to remain in the hallway for he wasn't allowed to sit among the white audience. Becoming licensed to preach in the Apostolic Faith Church, he answered a call to a small mission church in Los Angeles. After two weeks, he was expelled from the church but not deterred. Finding other venues to preach in, he

---

1. Bill Clinton's first childhood home, Hope, where Clinton was born and raised to about four, is a little over twenty miles from Stamps, where Maya Angelou spent many of her formative childhood years.

eventually ended up in a run-down building on Azusa Street. Seymour kept preaching and then fire came from the sky, world-views turned upside down, dams burst open and the Azusa Street revival was a Pentecostal prayer-shout heard around the world. Some people think of revivals lasting a week or two. This one went on for about nine years. It was characterized by speaking in tongues, healings, inter-racial audiences, and an emphasis on world evangelism.

Needless to say, the established churches, for the most part, looked down their noses at these enthusiastic and noisy Pentecostals who often came from the wrong side of society's railroad tracks. The Pagan philosophers made similar criticisms of the early Christians. But what can't be denied is that Pentecostalism grew like wild fire on the plains. Parham's influence diminished after he was charged with sodomy. And Seymour at the end of his life, preached to smaller and smaller audiences. But Pentecostalism continued its rapid growth and in a few short years had spread to Africa, Asia, India, Europe, and the Middle East.

As one can imagine, in a religious movement that emphasized dramatic emotional experiences and not well-constructed theological thought, sensationalism, aberrations, and abuses abounded. One's mind naturally drifts to literary allusions of preachers who pound the pulpit by day and the bed by night. In time, among some of these preachers and laity, a realization broke through that there needed to be some sort of structure, some sort of accountability, some way to sift the genuine from the carnival barkers. Eudorus N. Bell, a University of Chicago graduate who was pastoring a Pentecostal church in Malvern, Arkansas, sent out a clarion call that the time had come. More than 300 preachers and lay people from twenty different states and several foreign countries gathered in Hot Springs from April 2–14, 1914, and forged a new denomination: The General Counsel of the Assemblies of God.[2] Bell became the first General Superintendent. They gathered for multiple reasons which included the need to join together to further expand their missionary efforts, to establish Bible Colleges, and to develop identity, unity, and discipline. In 1916, due to the spread of the Oneness movement, the fledgling denomination adopted a statement of Trinitarian faith: "The Fundamental Truths." The first headquarters was

---

2. The history of the Assemblies of God considered by many to be the standard is Menzies *Anointed to Serve*. For a very accessible treatment of that history, see Blumhofer's *The Assemblies of God*.

briefly in Findlay, Ohio. In 1915, it moved to Saint Louis and in 1918, it came to Springfield, Missouri, where it remains to this day.

The Assemblies of God was counter-cultural in its formation in more ways than just glossolalia. Due to its theological conviction that the Holy Spirit is no respecter of persons, from its very beginnings, they allowed women to be ministers and exercise their ministry as evangelists and missionaries. This is quite striking when one considers that the United States did not even allow women to vote nationally until 1920. Women were not allowed to be pastors in the Assemblies until 1935 but that was still years ahead of most mainline denominations. The struggle for racial equality within the AG took a much longer trajectory, which is quite surprising when one considers the impact within the Pentecostal world of William Seymour.[3]

From its beginnings, the Assemblies of God had a strong commitment to pacifism. As the decades accumulated and, as it felt pressure from the surrounding military drum beat of a nation constantly at war, it compromised its position. The capitulation was so dramatic that by the 1970's and 80's, some quarters of the Assemblies were positively hawkish: all in support of motherhood, apple pie, baseball, and modern warfare. The theological dissonance created is piercingly painful when, on one side of the brain one has such a concern for the lost that one sends missionaries all over the world and yet, on the other, in times of nationalistic fervor, strongly supports the military industrial complex while unsaved and saved die through indiscriminate aerial bombings.

Reinhold Niebuhr was a tamed cynic, and I hope the same can be said about me. After reading this section, I realized an addendum is needed. It's easy to laugh at the excesses of religious zealots. They make it far too accessible to enjoy the sport of spotting the ludicrous. During my sojourn with the Pentecostals, I became an avid reader of a satirical magazine called *The Wittenburg Door* and devoured every issue. But the existence of the absurd does not categorically deny other realities. Just because someone, on some street corner, who obviously fell off his meds tells you that he is Moses, doesn't mean that Moses didn't actually walk on the planet thousands of years ago. Just because someone informs you that he is Moses doesn't rule out that Moses still lives in some other reality. For orthodox Christians,

3. Those familiar with the Caucasian-Americans bolting from the Church of God in Christ due to its leadership positions being dominated by African-Americans and consequently founding the Assemblies of God are not surprised at all. For a helpful article on this see Pete "Interracial Aspects of the Pentecostal Movement."

the Transfiguration, as recorded in the Synoptic Gospels, assures us that he does. Just because deluded individuals roam the land doesn't rule out that God is active in our world. Sometimes fire falls from the sky. Sometimes Otherness blinds like an inferno. It did for Moses, Elijah, Peter, James, and John, for Symeon the New Theologian, for Blaise Pascal, and I suspect, though I can't prove, for that Oxbridge Evangelist, C.S. Lewis, who was cagey like a fox. But of course, he somewhat had to be for he lived in a milieu which had bowed down at the altar of logical positivism.

III. Sounds of an Approaching Slow Train

What I also failed to mention in the previous section, is all the great friendships I developed during this time. When you entered into the Pentecostal world, you were initiated into a whole new language. All of a sudden, people who were your friends were also your "brothers or sisters in the Lord." You also developed a greater sense of intimacy with Jesus. He wasn't just the Lord of the Universe spending his time keeping asteroids from crashing into the earth, but also somehow had time for every one of us. He was now my closest friend. In the Pentecostal realm, God is ever so near, concerned about every hair or lack thereof.

During this time, my world was baptized anew. It was, as the Jesuit Gerard Manley Hopkins wrote so long ago, charged with God's grandeur. At times, it appeared like light dancing off crumbled up and unfolded aluminum foil. Sometimes when the wind blew, I was sure it was the Holy Spirit. Sometimes I felt like I could walk right into eternity. It affected me like those childhood days when I would climb onto the roof of Grandma's well house, reach over to the nearby tree, ascend the branches till I got to the metal roof of the shed and there I would lie as I watched the skies turn from blue to streaks of red, yellow, and a light purplish haze. As the patches of color formed in the sky, it looked almost like a highway so near yet unreachable. While hanging out with the Pentecostals, it seemed like a bridge had been built to that which was once inaccessible. I looked around, at this juncture in my life, and felt sadness for all those who didn't seem to delight in God's love.

It wasn't the Pentecostal preachers that moved me. Some of them were incredibly good and godly people; others were quite annoying. Some were downright weird; others were shady. A friend of mine once said, "If someone starts talking to me about Jesus in the first five minutes of meeting me, I reach my hands around to protect my wallet and my belt buckle." That's actually a sound maxim to live by. Some of those Pentecostal polyester wearing preachers made slimy used car salesmen look good. The Pentecostal world is a world of sensationalism and preachers develop reputations and salaries based on the number of people they can manipulate to the altar. I grew to hate the song "Just as I am" as I heard it played way too many times. Some of those preachers dispensed easy digestible religious formulas like banks mail out credit cards to the poor, like drugs dealers give out samples of crack on the street. Some of them peddled in dispensationalism which I thought nonsensical. Some believed Satan created dinosaur bones to tempt humanity to reject creationism.[4] Seriously, how could someone be that delusional? Some repeated the long dead Archbishop James Ussher's date of creation, 4004 BC. That seventeenth century Irish archbishop stated that not only did the world begin in that year but qualified it further by insisting that it happened on the date of October 23 at 6 pm. There was so much nonsense coming from those pulpits that I tuned it out and also started to ponder how it could be done better.

What I tuned in for was the music. I loved the music: the guitars, the drums, the beautiful women vocalists wearing a tad too much makeup, the pop tunes, and the easily sung lyrics. Some might say that adding 'the beautiful women' in the previous sentence is gratuitous. But if your church life consisted of men droning on through the mass, machine-like, then one might begin to appreciate how a change of scenery was nice. One should not underestimate aesthetic evangelism on the minds of eighteen-year-olds.

Though I loved the easy sung praise tunes, they didn't impact me anywhere as much as the music from an unlikely source. My good fortune is that the intensification of my religious quest came about the same time period as that of the denizen of Minnesota, Robert Allen Zimmerman. The high priest of my religious journey was not creepy Jimmy Swaggart or deeply misguided and materialistic Jim Bakker. My high priest was Bob Dylan. I knew every song, every lyric of *Slow Train Coming*. It was released August 1979, the beginning of the Fall semester of my freshman year. It didn't matter if you were an ambassador, a gambler, a heavyweight champion, or a socialite; still you had to serve someone. And I wailed on "I Believe in You" resonating with those lines about frowns and being driven

---

4. For any reader enduring sermons like I once heard and would like some helpful resources on the area of Christianity and Science see works by Francis Collins, John Lenox, Alister McGrath, and John Polkinghorne.

from town. There is no doubt that my religious journey was not welcomed by a great majority of my family. Mom was certain that I would end up in some airport dressed in a white sheet, selling flowers, and chanting while playing a tambourine. Other members of my family also cast scorn upon my aspirations. But that didn't matter because, as I bounced over dirt roads in my Datsun pickup, at ever so rapid rates of speed, Bob Dylan and I were singing together about being shown the door, being told not to come back any more. My voice, which I trained to be as nasal as Dylan's, bounced off the walls of the cab and out the window to the trees.

Arkansas Tech University, a suitcase college, had a good number of students who returned home every weekend. But a fair number also stayed and what complicated the situation was that the Greeks lived in the dorms. ATU had no fraternity or sorority houses. My floor had some rather loud Kappa Alphas. They struck me as kids raised by helicopter parents of Southern Baptist leanings. And I never understood why so many of them complained about the cafeteria food. For me, the cafeteria was a place of wonder; all this food was prepared for you and you simply picked up a tray and got it. Anytime you wanted, iced tea was available, waiting for an opportunity to quench thirst. But those helicopter offspring, here they were for the first time in their lives free from their parents controlling ways, and the hand-cuffs of their religious repression fell away: amazing grace indeed. They had no clue how to handle their freedom, alcohol, drugs, studies, or any other number of issues. I found no allure in their stumbling around stupidity. Having gotten my passport stamped from my childhood journeys, I had no desire to return to that land of intoxication. It's amazing how drunken undergraduates can find themselves to be clever, sexy, or athletic when to the sober they look in need of coffee. I prayed that none of them would fall out of the third-floor window of Turner Hall. Not everyone who lived on Third South behaved in that way. There were scholars on our floor with ear plugs busy preparing for medical or law school. Sprinkled into the mix, for good measure, were a few other religious zealots like myself, peppered in there by God, or by the universe's sense of irony.

I loved Arkansas Tech. It was so much easier to be a Christian there than at the school I transferred to after my freshman year. To this day, I look back on the decision to leave Tech with regret. ATU was great. There was clarity about it. You knew who you needed to witness to; the ones covered with their own drool, reeking of Budweiser, or of Willie Nelson's favorite herbal medicine. There was beauty in that simplicity. It was so easy to find compassion for them; so easy to be able to say, "Don't let this become a habit or the king of your life. I grew up in chaos. Don't make it your home. Free yourself and find your stability in the rock named Jesus."

Though there was so much good about this time of my life, I have to admit that not a small number of people experienced me as insufferable, self-righteous, and arrogant. Certainly, a fair number perceived me as too much of a prude for my own good. Martin Luther is quoted as saying, "We are all mere beggars showing other beggars where to find bread." My evangelism operated from a position of superiority. My religious haughtiness painfully revealed just what a beggar I was. I just, at that time, didn't have eyes to see.

IV. Bridges Crossed and Burnt

A few of my friends attended Evangel University in Springfield, Missouri which is a liberal arts college owned by the Assemblies of God. Some of you are thinking: liberal arts and the AG, isn't that an oxymoron? My response most days is "yep." It certainly brought its own tension. My friends encouraged me to transfer and I did so without ever visiting the campus. Back then I deemed it as a step of faith. Now I would declare it an absurd and poor excuse for not doing one's homework. Loading up my Datsun pickup, I headed out, crossing the Ada Mills Bridge to get to Highway 21, going north to Springfield. Upon arriving on campus in the Fall of 1980 and observing all the run down, vintage World War II barracks, I began to doubt. In 1954, the Assemblies of God acquired the old O'Reilly General Hospital from the US Army. During the Second World War more than one hundred thousand patients passed through that hospital. As we sat in a classroom that was said to be the old operating room, we wondered, how many of them didn't make it? Perhaps ghosts haunted the hallways. In the winter, the buildings were cold, drafty, and they creaked.

One could argue that from its very foundation there was too close a bond between God, country, military, church, and college. Evangel opened for classes on September 1, 1955, in the old army white frame wooden buildings. Fielding a football team for the first time in the mid to late 1970s is what really put Evangel on the map among the Assemblies of God schools. Some old guard Pentecostals feared that the school capitulated to masculine Christianity and the result would be falling academic standards and cheerleaders getting a bun in the oven. A longer view would instruct that eighteen years down the road this could be a potential boon for enrollment. The football program was one more thing which differentiated Evangel from its sister college across town, Central Bible College (CBC). I didn't like stepping on CBC's grounds; it seemed to me an alien world. One day while walking through a dorm on CBC's campus, I passed a room where a polyester suit wearing preacher practiced his preaching in front of a mirror. I know this is an unfair judgment on my part, but he seemed to reek of a stale, superficial holiness, so prone in a denomination which misled their young to treat their own humanity with disdain.

CBC cast its holiness stare on EU. For many students raised in the AG, Evangel was like that moment when the fog clears and one beholds a beautiful, clear, mountain day. By attending Evangel, some of their rigid dogmatism of their local Pentecostal churches began to give way. At Evangel, each student was required to take *Essential Christianity* and read works like Art Holmes' *All Truth is God's Truth*. All of a sudden, chains fell off of some students, and they no longer feared that learning would automatically result in the loss of faith. Now they were instructed to glorify God with their art, music, literature, and science. For some that was as big a revolution as the Copernican.

Initially, I too reveled in being in a place where everyone loved Jesus. Mandatory chapel was no burden my first semester there. As time accumulated, it became so. The chaplain, a kind old soul, invited in to preach too many saw dust trail wannabes. One wonders just how many of those traveling evangelists one can listen to before one takes a bottle to the brain. Evangel, as already mentioned, had a reputation in some sectors of the AG for being a liberal bastion of renegade students who listened to rock music—who snuck alcohol on campus—who engaged in the devil's playground of hedonism. Almost every blasted guest preacher/evangelist tried to convert us. There were so many altar calls; they became cliché. But for the evangelists, having a large response to the altar call became a part of their promotional bios. It struck me with no small amount of irony that the student body of this supposed liberal bastion in a straw poll voted by over 85 percent for Ronald Reagan for president in 1980. Somehow, they didn't get the memo that Jimmy Carter was actually a practicing Christian who tried to reflect Jesus' values in the limited use of military force. The part of the chapel I loved most was the music; it was far more captivating, at that time in my life, than Gregorian chants.

There is so much good in my life, as a result of my attending Evangel, that it is ironic I am so conflicted about the institution; first, the good, and later the disillusionment which led to the mixed emotions. The great good of Evangel is all the friendships I made. Evangel had some absolutely wonderful students. In fact, I would hold them up against any other academic institution I attended in terms of what matters most in life: having kind hearts. Some of them remained lifelong friends and some of them sadly due to moving, career, family, and the passing of time have fallen away, casualties of a busy, transitory life. But I'm grateful for how they enriched my life. The student body came from all over the United States and the world, and there was diversity of lived experiences. From its beginnings, the AG was a missionary movement and, in a short period of time, had sent missionaries to the metaphorical four corners of the world. Those missionaries wanted their children educated, by and large, in AG schools in the US, and Evangel received a fair number of them.

My transition to Evangel was not difficult as I already had friends there. I began as a business major but, after the first semester, changed to biblical studies. The course of my life had been dramatically altered and yet, in so many ways, remained the same. When I moved into Krause Third South, the room across the hall had three students. Normally a dorm room was shared by only two students but construction on the new dorm, Lewis Hall, ran behind schedule and for the first few weeks of school, accommodation had to be made. One of those intended for Lewis Hall was named Philos (Phil). Had the dormitory's construction schedule not been delayed, I might never have become friends with my temporary neighbor. I might never have become friends with someone whose friendship impacted me profoundly and also contributed to my final disillusionment with the AG. Phil, from a suburban community outside of Washington, DC, arrived at Evangel with a large 8 x 10 framed photo of his fiancé that his roommates said he kissed each morning when he got up. He was hopelessly in love with her.

From my Arkansas perspective, Phil was sophisticated. He was fun, loved to laugh, and didn't take school too seriously. He also had a great sense of fashion. Though we were close friends for over three years, friends as close of brothers, what he would not tell me, though he told others, was that he was struggling with his sexuality. Not until after I graduated did he finally find the courage to tell me that he was gay. He was afraid of my reaction, and if I'm honest, he had a valid concern as I was more zealous about my religion than Phil. I was quite judgmental, at that time in my life, with those I believed morally weak.[5] No matter how far we travel from our own genesis, we can't outrun our parents' shadows. Though we try, we find they remain with us and we react to their foibles and failures with either judgment, emulation, or some strange concoction of both. Furthermore, complicating the whole issue, back then, was the perception that a practicing homosexual would be immediately expelled from the school.

The Assemblies of God offered judgment and seemed white and black about the particular words of Jesus they chose to enforce. Phil loved his home AG church, and the pastor of that church was the one who guided him to Evangel. When Phil finally found the courage to share with the pastor and his wife about his sexual identity, the pastor's wife told him that he was demon possessed. They attempted to expel the gay demon from Phil's soul.

I've known few people in my life as kind as Phil. He was certainly kinder than I will ever be. My mom, on more than one occasion, said that there must be piss and vinegar flowing through my veins. All I can say to that is, like Walker Percy, I think nice is overrated. Phil, being kind and sincere, sat there while the preacher and his wife committed religious malpractice. At that point, Phil would have gladly had the alternate lifestyle demon sent away from his life. How much easier that would have been than living in a society and a religious culture that ridiculed and demonized him. Conforming to a society's expectations by marrying the woman he loved would have been a cake-walk compared to the *Via Dolorosa* awaiting him. He sat there hurt, confused, and broken.

If something threatens the conventionality of some AG folks, they quickly label it from "the pit of hell." If there were anything that I was exposed to in those years that I believed came from the pit of hell, it was that awful, painful sound one heard when Jimmy Swaggart sang while playing the piano. Now that was truly hell on earth. The irony of all of this is that, back then, Phil would have gladly labeled his own behavior as sinful. He just wanted to know why the church discriminates regarding which sin it chooses to enforce. Homosexuality is listed as a sin in the Scriptures, but so too is gluttony. Why is it that homosexuality gets you labeled as demon possessed, but obese AG preachers (and for that matter Methodist preachers)

---

5. Any sense of moral superiority I felt as a young person dissipated under the weight of my food addictions, a struggle I have longed to gain victory over but have failed again and again.

get to keep their credentials? Why is it that at every church wide pot luck supper, no one gets in a frenzy over plates heaped full with a week's worth of calories?[6] Greed is listed as a sin in the Scriptures.[7] Why is it that the Assemblies TV evangelists like Jimmy Swaggart and Jimmy Bakker were treated as favored sons even as they manipulated little old ladies into giving away their limited financial resources? They were treated as favored sons even as they lived in palatial mansions. My disillusionment with the AG began long before Phil told me about his sexuality, but his experiences of rejection certainly cemented it.

Because Phil didn't want to be gay, because he tried everything in the world not to be gay including having sex with his fiancée, because he feared that he was evil due to his longings, the once simplistic positions I held about homosexuality crumbled like an ancient wall whose mortar deteriorated from being weather beaten. I reevaluated my position on homosexuality. Prior to knowing Phil, I thought of it as some kind of horrible abomination. When he told me, my first emotion was not compassion, but anger that he didn't tell me three years before. Looking backwards, I'm stunned that I somehow felt entitled to that knowledge. As the days gave way to weeks and the weeks to months, I realized that he was hard-wired that way. It wasn't a genetic malfunction. He wasn't demon possessed. He was born that way. Phil and I stayed in contact through the years. He was one of the groomsmen in my wedding and about ten years after that, he became sick and, in time, died.

Another friend who greatly impacted me was Mikros, a missionary kid (MK) from the Caribbean. His roommate, who I also became friends with, was a MK from the same place. One of the great heresies of the Pentecostal world at this time was the prosperity gospel. Kenneth Hagin and Kenneth Copeland were the chief apostles of this materialistic movement seeking a hostile takeover of a first-century Jewish carpenter of humble origins. We referred to this heretical movement as Copenhagen. They proclaimed an appealing message that if you just believe Jesus' promises in your heart and confess them with your mouth, keeping all doubt away, then God will give you the desires of your heart. The logic goes that God wants to give his children good things so just keep confessing and he will give

6. There are many references to Gluttony in the Scriptures. A few of them are: Philippians 3:19, Proverbs 23:20–21, Proverbs 28:7.

7. Jesus spoke about the dangers of greed more than any other sin. The New Testament is replete with warnings against it. A few examples are: Luke 3:14, Luke 12: 15–21, Matthew 6:24, John 12:6, James 5:1–6.

you a new Mercedes, a multi-million-dollar house, and a fat bank account. Plus, as demonstrated by the evangelists themselves, a never-ending supply of jet planes. Of course, this is an evidence-based theology and if you fail to look and live like a billionaire then the problem resides in your lack of faith. My friends told me stories of TV evangelists who descended on their small island in their jet planes and stayed on the ground only long enough for the TV crews to take some pictures and video to emotionally manipulate American audiences into giving monies to their sham charities.

The Pentecostal religious world is a Wild, Wild West where for some practitioners' avarice, pride, and lasciviousness are normal practices of the "vocation." Back then, a group of us biblical studies majors were counter-cultural, wanting to remove the western cultural alterations and get back to the core of the Gospel, to strip away from it the many different ways that institutions corrupt it. Burning idealists for Jesus, we were shocked that the mascot of our university was a Crusader. We were equally scandalized by the name of the student union, the Joust. I read somewhere that Evangel conducted a survey of its alumni asking them what they thought of their mascot and the name of the student union and whether it should be changed. I don't remember getting that survey, but the vast majority of the alumni voiced strongly that they wanted it to remain. They were proud it connoted going forth as conquerors, citing as a rationale that it instructs us to be bold for the faith.

So many years ago, we, as young burning idealists, wondered what kind of truth Evangel proclaimed, the kind achieved by the end of the sword or perhaps a take-off on the old golden rule: he or she with the most gold makes the rules. We desired to become missionaries emulating Christ, pouring ourselves out in service, and our school celebrated the medieval Pope's armies sacking Constantinople, murdering their fellow Christians, and destroying priceless church treasures. Here we were in a school that utilized imagery celebrating European militants who unjustly invaded the Holy Land. And this was not Rome's first trip there, as little baby Jesus also lived under the tyranny of the Empire. The mascot and the name of the student union was the antithesis of a biblical understanding of mission. Evangel had taught us too well and now we were calling into question its practices. The crusaders and the joust were images not of kenosis but of blunt use of power. They might as well have called the student union the Cardinal of Seville's Fun House. The president of the school gave us biblical studies majors a tongue lashing one day, informing us that everywhere he went, people told him how arrogant his theology majors were. They gave us sharp tools and then asked us to beat them into dullness.

Another lifelong friend made at Evangel was Andreas, a Canadian from Mississauga, who was a philosophy and literature major. Andreas introduced me to the music of Bruce Cockburn, and I learned about Yonge Street, the coldest night of the year, and I started wondering where all the lions are. I feared Evangel domesticated them. Dissecting the preachers' sermons in the chapel, desperately looking for structure and some interpretation of the text, we found instead a lot of eisegesis. We analyzed the president of the college's words and actions and found him, in our humble opinions, wanting. We started paying attention to who got kicked out of the college for drinking infractions and who didn't. The children and grandchildren of the old guard AG denominational leaders appeared to get preferential treatment, not that we actually were in possession of any first-hand institutional knowledge. We paid attention to the seal of the university, especially the big word in the center, TRUTH. A university built upon truth is what the seal connoted, but we began to notice the difference between the ideal and the realism which drove the institution.

I spent the summer before my senior year backpacking in Europe. My disenfranchisement with the AG was complete, but my faith in God resolute. Still having a passion for those who didn't know Jesus, I engaged in cold call evangelism on the streets of Wiesbaden and in other places. The summer in Europe changed me for I realized that the world is a far more complicated place than what Arkansas, California, and Missouri had prepared me for. Now it was clear that the simple answers given by so many Christians were inadequate. I appreciated my time at L'Abri in Huémoz. Rome also greatly impacted me: The Colosseum and pondering the poverty on the streets around the Vatican. Hoping that luck would be on my side and that I would bump into the Pope, I walked around the Vatican, again and again, but it never happened. I so wanted to ask him, "How come my father was excluded from the means of grace?"

When I returned for my senior year at Evangel, I didn't want to be there. My girlfriend broke up with me the semester before; she started dating the son of a TV evangelist. I wasn't interested in my studies, yet for some reason I spent a great deal of time day dreaming about pursing a graduate degree at the University of Edinburgh. Having been changed by conceptual revolutions and by my experiences and the experiences of others, I knew that there was no way I could ever join an Assemblies church, nor could I ever be one of their preachers. I was a biblical study major without a denomination. Now that's a promising future, eh? Everything pointed in the direction of quitting and returning home, but to do so would mean admitting to my family that I made a mistake. Since that was not going to happen, I went through the motions. It was a miserable year but, even in that, God is good for I was given two great gifts: Twila Edwards and the Bohican House.

Edwards, an amazing professor, introduced me to the imaginative and rational world of C.S. Lewis. In Lewis, I found a path that navigated the dark and the light, the mysterious and the rational. The second gift is that I was allowed to live off campus. Lorne, a MK friend of mine (we were co-chairs of the student mission organization) lived in his mother's house with a couple of other Evangel students. The reason why this was allowed, despite Evangel's rule that single students needed to live on campus, was that Lorne's dad had died in the mission field. The rent supplemented her missionary resources as she remained engaged in the field. Lorne and his housemates fastened big Greek wooden letters to the front of the house to the delight of the neighbors, I'm sure. The Greek letters were Beta, Phi, and Omega which stood for Bohicans forever. Bohican was an acronym for a philosophy of life they espoused; Bend over here it comes again. I need to emphasize that this did not reflect a practice of theirs but a philosophy that the AG and the world was out to get them. My youthful cynicism found a home in the Bohican house. Though I have never returned to Evangel University for an alumni reunion, if an invitation ever arrived for a Bohican House Reunion, you better believe I would book a flight. The great shame of it is that I can no longer fit in my old Bohican sweatshirt.

The Evangel University I write about is a snapshot from the past.[8] I haven't been on campus in more than twenty-five years and the last time I was there, my wife informed me that my suppressed hostility came out in rudeness to some poor innocent secretary. I know very little about the university now. But the university of the past was a place of great promise and deep disappointment; a place that valued and rewarded conformity to conservative religious and political views. Those who failed to fit the mold were often treated as outsiders. But I've got to tell you that Evangel had some great outliers.

8. These etchings of the Assemblies of God are also snapshots of a distant past. I haven't been in an AG church since before I left Evangel (with the exception of a wedding) and have not kept up with the changes in the denomination.

Some evangelist blew into town getting a great number of students up in arms as if they were about to fall into hell. During this week of spiritual renewal, the evangelist convinced them to bring all their sinful rock albums, romance novels, and the tools of the devil and pile them up in front of the cafeteria. There was going to be a real live twentieth century bonfire of the vanities. I was told, though I didn't see them myself, that there were also birth control devices there. I imagine some efficient school employee quickly removed them. Of course, the plus side of that is that in eighteen years, that bonfire of the vanities could lead to an increase in school enrollment.

Walking by the pile of records, a friend noticed some great rock albums. Being an ethical young man who knew that stealing was wrong, he returned to his room and gathered some old Imperial, Amy Grant, and Gaither albums. Walking back to the sin heap, he exchanged them for albums by Kansas, Chicago, and the Rolling Stones.

V. ICE CUBES IN A LIQUOR GLASS

No one put a gun to my head and said that I had to attend an Assemblies of God school. I chose to do that. In fact, the choice I made was, as already mentioned, disapproved of by my family which was one more reason why admitting defeat didn't come easy. Truly, I regretted not transferring back to ATU. It was clear after the first year that the journey from Roman Catholicism to the Assemblies of God was a bridge too far. Compounding mistakes is an art form I have mastered.

As I reread the previous sections, it struck me that some of my bellyaches about the AG are like complaining about a squirrel having a tail and jumping from branch to branch in a tree. When squirrels do what squirrels do, is that their fault? Some might ask, "Why are you angry at the zebra for having stripes?" That is a fair observation. The Assemblies were who they were long before I ever chose to associate with them. Long before I knew of them, they had a lengthy history of being leery of foreign influence. They were busy creating their own identity and their own institutions many decades before I was born. Their DNA is one of emotion, sensationalism, altar calls, and competing claims of divine revelation.

The anger I possess is truly anger at me for not acting when I knew what I needed to do. It wouldn't take a rocket scientist to figure out that I didn't fit in there. One time, upon entering a friend's room, I saw him sitting at his desk with scissors beside him and a magnifying glass in his right hand. Bending over his desk, he stared at a magazine ad of ice cubes in a glass of liquor. Asking him what he was doing, he replied that he was looking for subliminal faces of demons in the melting ice. Startled, I inquired, "You're kidding right?" He was sober serious. His heart was good as gold, and he was sincere as any. I counted him as a trusted friend. Yet there he was, looking for demons in whiskey ads. I thought his melting ice cubes were, in reality, a Rorschach test.

I remember having arguments with people over what to do if someone were about to die of starvation. Do you first tell them about Jesus and have them recite the sinner's prayer, or do you feed them? To the normal, sane person the answer is obvious, but in the rarified world of the AG it became an argument of the Full Gospel versus the Social Gospel. And for many, the Social Gospel was code for pissing away Jesus, accommodating him to the world.

I spent a great deal of time wishing I had never transferred to Evangel. I was an outsider in a closely-knit relationship world. At the beginning of the semester when the professor was taking attendance, he or she would stop and ask if the student was related to this AG preacher, professor, or one of the chosen ones who ran the denomination. Standing outside all of that and grateful I didn't grow up in that world, I wondered what in God's name was I doing there. What was I doing sitting in a drafty, army, cracker box of a building listening to a world-view I found too restrictive?

Evangel had more than its fair share of brilliant professors and students, and those liberal Protestants who look down their noses at them do so to their own peril. The problem is and was not a problem of brilliance. The problem, for the Assemblies of God back then, was stranger-danger; fear of ideas that question old guard assumptions, fear of a world which is constantly changing. That fear led previous AG generations to build a Christian cultural ghetto with their own books, music, schools, publishing houses, and TV and radio ministries.

I never will forget the stir on campus when some old guard Pentecostal person of some stature complained that the Christian music in the jukebox in the Joust was too worldly. Now mind you, it didn't play any secular music. But the religious music that was played was just not the right kind of religious music. They taught us that all truth is God's truth, but they attempted to limit and sanitize what we could consume.

One day, in the Assemblies of God Graduate School Library, back in the days when it was in the blue building (the Assemblies of God Vatican), I came across a book of biblical criticism containing a warning that it was to be read only by professors and not to be read by impressionable young minds. It was a throw back from a day long gone and yet it remained in my mind as a metaphor of that time.

I left Evangel having been given the gifts of thoughtful and thought-provoking professors, and some amazing friends, some who left the AG and some who have remained. I also left Evangel knowing for sure two things: sometimes fire falls from the sky, and I was not called to pitch my tent in the land of the AG.

Chapter Three

Rebuilding the Concept of Church

I. Wondering about Lions

Reality came crashing down my last semester at Evangel. What does one do with a degree in Biblical Studies? IBM wasn't lining up outside my door and that was a good thing because I didn't have a resume prepared. Not looking for a career, I didn't panic, possessing instead deep intuitions that everything was going to be ok. *The Lance*, the student newspaper at Evangel, quoted my serenity in the midst of other seniors frantically engaging in the paper shuffle. Though not troubled about it, my mom's never-ending questions about my plans (or lack thereof) for the future got old. To this day, I don't know why I didn't apply for the Peace Corps. That would have been a great fit, but I never gave it a thought. I entertained, for a while, attending the University of Tunisia for language school and even wrote away for an application. Eventually I settled upon applying to Western Kentucky University for graduate school. WKU was unique among state university religion departments as it was staffed largely with evangelicals and former evangelicals. They offered me an out-of-state tuition waiver and a graduate assistantship.

Time had moved on. Exhausted by organized religion, I turned down the offer to WKU as I couldn't see how one more degree in religion could possibly help. I never lost my faith in Jesus. My confidence in humanity's ability to organize religious communities was deeply shaken. Tired of religious conversations, church attendance, sinful denominations, and polyester- wearing preachers, I headed home after graduation to work for Mom and regroup. If I had given that any thought, I would have realized that though I'm her last child, I'm a whole lot like her. We were both highly opinionated, bull-headed, fiercely independent, and not especially gifted at being told what to do. She gave me directions for tasks to complete, and I, constantly, suggested different methodologies for their execution. Though she continually drew my attention to whose signature was on my check, I pretended not to see or hear. It's a shame that I hadn't been a drummer in a rock band. That would have given some validity to my lack of response. This arrangement lasted less than a month, and it became apparent that I needed to return to Springfield.

Calling up a friend who was tired of living in a cramped basement apartment with nosy landlords who were constantly looking through his trash (they were old-line AG and fretted that their renter might be drinking), he readily agreed to rent a two-bedroom apartment with me. Finding a part-time job at Morrison's Cafeteria as the beverage person, my claim to fame was that my iced tea glasses didn't sweat. Enrolling at Southwest Missouri State University, I pursued course work in cultural anthropology.

When asked to recount my spiritual journey to various groups, I normally deal with this excursion with one sentence: "After coming to the realization that I couldn't save souls, I decided to preserve human culture." The actual reasoning process was a little more subversive, and had its roots in my student days at Evangel. At this time, in mission discussions, conversations were had about foreign governments closing their doors to US missionaries. One way to enter into other lands was to have a skill valued by that government. Through my network of MK friends, I got to know Raleigh Farrell who formerly taught anthropology at Washington State University, but then was teaching at the Assemblies of God Theological Seminary. Farrell, an expert in Taiwanese aboriginal peoples and languages, graciously gave time to discussions with Evangel students who wanted to explore anthropology careers.

This time in Springfield, marked by two different worlds (SMSU and Morrison's Cafeteria) bore fruit. For too long I had inhabited a closed religious world which was not as isolated as a monastery yet proved removed from the everyday world. Evangel claimed to be preparing us to go out and reach this world for Christ yet they kept us separated from the vernacular of ordinary lives. Thus, we were enculturated with Christian music, language, art and were not given trusty bridges to cross that would enable us to effectively reach those who we assumed were lost. Into the world of Morrison's Cafeteria, I entered wide-eyed. Though tempted to take notes like a good ethnologist, I feared I would have stuck out more awkwardly than I already did. In this world, drama was afoot. The cook had impregnated one of the waitresses and was having an affair with another. It was all talked about much like the weather. At Evangel, I only would have seen something like this watching a daytime soap opera, but here it all was in plain view. The pregnant waitress frequently cried while the older waitresses comforted her and gave icy dagger stares to the one who had captured the cook's eye. And she pranced around the dining room as if she wore a shield of Teflon. In this world, a social hierarchy held. The cook rated above the beverage boy. He made more money, and the managers were of a different class. Evangel had not prepared me for any of this although my childhood certainly did.

Once again, I was surrounded by people living hard-scrabble lives; people who largely were not given the benefit of a post-secondary education. Economically marginal, they carried modest dreams hoping to gain enough money in tips and what not to pay for a car, a rented house, and some groceries. Though I felt completely at home with them, I didn't know how to reach them with the Gospel. By them, I mean the unchurched. Some of those waitresses were deeply religious and knew the Bible better than I did. What they knew about me was that I had graduated the May before with a Biblical Studies degree and was now filling glasses up with tea. Some were annoyed with me as if somehow, I was mocking their world by working there. And some of the waitresses thought "the Bible major student was cute as he could be" and enjoyed pinching part of my anatomy as they passed by. This too was an education of sorts.

Though still technically Roman Catholic, I functioned as a Jesus follower done with denominations and all church attendance ceased. I praised God by singing my way through Dylan's successive gospel albums: *Saved* and *Shot of Love*. I found God in the music. I expanded my musical canon adding the works of Bruce Cockburn and U2. Cynical of organized religion, I still read the Scriptures and prayed.

As the semester at SMSU wound down, feeling conflicted about my future course and whether I should close the door on the church once and for all, I opted for a prolonged retreat. Some members of my family registered consternation at this idea especially since the manager at Morrison's Cafeteria had invited me to become an assistant manager. This would have entailed going away to be trained in their management program. One family member said, "For once in your life get a real job." He said that not because I was a financial drain on the family for school or for my wanderings. I earned my own way. He said it because he was puzzled that I was taking a different path. Understanding the family's point of view, I wondered why didn't I just get on with it. But there was this nagging feeling and peace remained elusive. They worried and wanted the best for me, but I didn't feel good about leaving the church in my rearview mirror. Even though I felt discontented with it and disconnected from it, still the belief, hard-wired from my childhood, remained; the church is the bride of Christ. Feeling the need for time away to process this, I got a job at Ontario Pioneer Camp (OPC) in Port Sydney, Ontario. OPC is an Intervarsity year-round camp. Job is overstating it; I was a volunteer who was given room and board and, if I remember right, a small amount of money for beer and books.

January 1984, I headed to the North Country. Spending a week or two at Andreas's parents' house, I attended classes with him at the University of Toronto. After a never-ending supply of bookstores, coffeehouses, pubs, and libraries, I left the bright lights of Toronto behind and got on a bus heading north. After two and a half hours, it came to a stop. The driver told me I had arrived. My destination looked desolate. As I stepped off the bus into the snow, I looked around for signs of civilization. None were to be found. Darkness enveloped me and the only lights were the crisp stars in the sky and the far distant nightlights of houses separated by a frozen wasteland. Today, there might be a Taco Bell across the street from where I stood, but not that night. I had never felt so alone. I sat down on my suitcase and waited.

Those fifteen, twenty, or twenty-five minutes were spent by taking note of how piercing the cold can be and doubting my decision to take some time for inward reflection, for resetting the internal compass. How can you recalibrate anything if you're nearly frozen to death? I started dreaming about the day when archaeologists digging deep into the tundra discovered the frozen man and his suitcase. Theories would rapidly develop as to what role the plastic Arkansas Razorback coffee mug played. Was it a chalice used for religious rituals? Obviously, they would deduce that frozen suitcase man was an animist who worshipped hogs. Speculations were interrupted by the lights of a pickup cutting the darkness.

As the truck came to a stop, a window rolled down, and the gregarious camp director asked me if I wanted a ride. At that point, frozen as I was, I would have climbed in the truck driven by almost anyone. Inquiring why

I wanted to come to camp in the middle of winter, he said, "spring and summer is so much nicer. And fall is glorious." I responded, "I can only imagine." As I began to thaw, I thought if I knew that cold could feel this bitterly jagged then I would have considered the Bahamas a better location for this spiritual journey into the wildness.

All the other workers at the camp had been there for at least half-a-year and were in the cabins and buildings around the cafeteria. I was placed on the other side of the lake in a little cabin. It was made of wood, painted brown with a reddish orange trim around the windows and the roof line. It had a stone fireplace. He said, "There's shovel inside and you'll need to shovel the snow off the roof every now and then so it doesn't collapse." My mind started. . .it can do that. . .the snow that is. . .crush a house. I verbalized my thoughts and he said, "oh yeah, snow's heavy."

I loved my Thoreau cabin. Every morning, while still dark outside, I put on my snow shoes, and walked across the frozen lake, listening to its groans, and the sounds of winter as the sun rose. It was majestic. Day by day, snow shoe sliding over snow shoe, I'd cross to the other side where the community awaited, singing a Cockburn song about the sun rising and the world surviving, a song about eternity and ecstasy, a song about lions at the door.

Days were spent working in the kitchen or cleaning the guest rooms as a fair number of school and church groups came in the middle of winter to conduct retreats. I learned how to cross-country ski but gained no proficiency in it. I reveled in the community of Americans and Canadians who had a deep love for OPC as they had all been campers there in their younger days. Regaling me with stories of how beautiful the lake is at summer time and how many campers are running all over the place, they insisted saying, "You've just got to stay here through the summer." I knew I couldn't stay that long. If I did, the relationships would deepen. If I stayed that long, I might never want to leave. And there was more traveling to do.

In my cabin, I began a philosophical work entitled, *Inherent Dualism*. After ten pages, my attention went elsewhere. In today's climate, somebody would have slapped a prescription on me for attention deficit disorder but, back then, I was labeled a "free-spirit." In the solitude of that cabin, I confronted my career uncertainty by not deciding. I would give myself some more time to study. Writing to the chair of the Department of Religion and Philosophy at Western Kentucky University, I apologized for turning down his most gracious offer of an assistantship and scholarship and inquired if I might be considered for the next year. In no time at all, he wrote back and it was all settled. In the fall of 1984, I would call Bowling Green my new place of residence. Sometime after that, realizing that I needed to earn some money for the fall, I returned home to work in the family business.

As the years have gone by, I have often been chided by my wife for telling people that I once lived in Canada. She says with much energy, "you didn't live there. You were just a visitor." Though I greatly appreciate her point of view, it doesn't connote how deeply I became attached to Port Sydney and Toronto in my two or three months spent in the North Country. I have returned to Toronto since then but have yet to make it back to Port Sydney. It remains on my bucket list.

II. Towers Tumbling Down

I remember where I was when I first heard the news. Standing at the hall phone in Krause Third South during my first year at Evangel, my brother, Tim, told me, in a voice full of joy and concern, that he had a son. James, born in the ambulance ride on Arkansas Highway 22 somewhere between Charleston and Central, came into the world premature weighing only two pounds. He would have to stay at Mercy Hospital in Fort Smith for some time. It turned out to be two and a half months. The doctor said that James was born with one kidney missing and the other sure to develop renal failure. They called it renal acidosis but those two words didn't come close to capturing the heartache. They said he wouldn't live past seven.

Watching James grow was a balm to our hearts. We worried about him and delighted in him. His facility with language was amazing. Rapidly, his mental acumen outstripped his peers even though his body lagged far behind. His brother Ben, born a year and nine months after James, was larger than James by the time Ben was three months' shy of two years. Easter 1984, hanging out with my brother and his family, I'm snapping shots of the boys getting ready for and hunting Easter Eggs. There's a picture of James dyeing an egg as it slips through his small hands. Another picture is of an Easter egg lodged at the top of the pocket of a pair of overhauls hanging on the clothes line. Locked in time is a picture of both boys bending over to smell some tulips in the yard. There's a picture of Ben, the sturdy, stout one, whose appetite got the best of him, standing there with an egg broken in two. Another picture is of James and Ben side by side with James' arm around his brother. I wonder how James, not yet four, processed that his younger brother was growing stronger and taller than him. He seemed to take it all in stride, but how could he really?

Working through the summer, preparing for WKU, I didn't notice the storm clouds in the sky. Around the first of August, a virus tore through James' fragile body. Dehydrated, throwing up, his parents raced him to the doctor who immediately sent him to Children's Hospital in Little Rock. The next day he slipped into a coma; eight days later, he died. Sometime in that terrible span of days, my brother took some water and baptized his first-born child. Worried that he might have not done it exactly correct, he did it again. After the end arrived, it all became a blur: the receiving of friends, the mass, the burial. Enduring the well-meant but vacuous words of people about God needing an angel felt like someone ripping off the skin. Through all the tears and the shock, I cried out like the psalmist of old, "My God, my God, why have you forsaken James, my family, and me?"

Less than a week later, I headed out east bound on I–40. My assistantship duties began on August 16 and I busied myself with the task at hand; meeting the chair of the department, and then the professors that I'd be working for: James Spiceland and E. Margaret Howe.[9] I graded exams for Intros to Philosophy, Logic, and New Testament. I also spent time in the library tracking down books and articles for them. Before I began, the Department Chair shared with me some information about both professors that he thought helpful and then he said that some of Dr. Howe's teaching assistants found working with her difficult. She had her expectations, for sure, but I found her to be sharp as a tack and had a great British sense of humor. As a Southerner, it took me a while to catch the drift.

My office cubicle, on the third floor of Cherry Hall, had a view of College Street. Down below stood the statue of Henry Hardin Cherry, founder of Bowling Green Normal School which in time became WKU. On my office walls hung a Rolling Stone magazine cover featuring Bob Dylan, a photo of Ernest Hemingway, a European magazine I picked up while backpacking which had U2 on the cover. Later, I added a program from an *Evening with James Thurber* done by the actor William Windom. Also taped to the wall was a flyer from when James Baldwin came to give a lecture. I never will forget (which demonstrates my total unawareness of some matters) at that

9. James Spiceland, a philosophy professor, was awarded the PhD from the University of Exeter (UK). His research in the philosophy of language was under the supervision of W.D. Hudson. E. Margaret Howe, a New Testament scholar, received the PhD from the University of Manchester (UK) and conducted her studies under the supervision of F.F. Bruce.

time, thinking to myself, as I sat in the auditorium, "Why is he so angry?" On top of this eclectic hall of portraits hung the Arkansas flag; back then, I had no clue what the fourth star represented.[10]

Of course, hidden beneath the smiles and my easy-going demeanor a storm raged. Days, weeks, and months went by in a blur, wondering what did the philosophical readings in Willard Quine and Alvin Plantinga have to do with the ugly reality that just happened?[11] Little James never had a chance. Let Neurath warp and revise his boat, I'm ready to blow my blasted craft up. All the sawdust trail evangelist wannabes, which paraded through Evangel's chapel hawking their snake oil potions, claiming miracles around every corner had nothing to say to me in that moment. I remember their stories of armies of angels delivering some missionaries from disaster and I wanted to know, I demanded to know, where was just one angel for James? Why was the all-powerful, all-loving God of the universe unmoved by my desperate prayers prayed while James was hooked up to medical contraptions, all my desperate prayers to the Lord of the Resurrection while the machines at Children's Hospital in Little Rock beeped and hummed?

During my age of grief, the multi-syllabic Pentecostals failed to speak to me, but the Existentialists resonated loudly. If I were pushed to tell you what moved me so deeply by their writings, I'd struggle. After a few moments, I'd stumble over something like this: Soren Kierkegaard's treatment of Abraham, Isaac, and the Leap of Faith gave me insight into the absurdity of the faith, a faith I continued to hold even despite the overwhelming mountain of evidence the opposition mounted. Sartre's *No Exit* showed me a depth of reality I didn't want to embrace. Camus' *The Outsider* and *The Plague* captured my imagination vividly portraying the heroic struggle against the capriciousness, indifference, and injustice of this world. Let

10. When the Arkansas flag was adopted by the state legislature in 1913, it had three stars on it signifying the nations to which it belonged: Spain, France, and the United States. In 1923, a fourth star was added representing the Confederate States of America.

11. Willard V. Quine (1908–2000), an analytic philosopher, held the Edgar Pierce Chair of Philosophy at Harvard University. Quine made significant contributions in logic, epistemology, philosophy of language, and philosophy of math. He was a pragmatist whose article "Two Dogmas of Empiricism," in the minds of many, put the prevailing philosophical school, empiricism, on the defensive. Quine was also an atheist. Alvin C. Plantinga, an analytic philosopher, is the John A.O'Brien Professor of Philosophy Emeritus at the University of Notre Dame and is currently the William H. Jellema Professor of Philosophy at Calvin College. Plantinga, one of the foremost Christian philosophers of religion, made substantial contributions in epistemology, philosophy of religion, Christian apologetics, and metaphysics. In 2017, Plantinga won the Templeton Prize.

those who trade in religious trite slogans and concepts in order to gain their palacious planes and houses plummet into the eighth level of hell. And then we can all pray for their redemption and, of course, our own.

The MA in philosophy required one to take a course in another discipline. In the spring semester, I took New Testament Theology with William Lane. Lane was a legend in the evangelical world of scholarship which was, in itself, painfully ironic. The unnamed, well-regarded, evangelical seminary, in which he was a tenured professor, turned its back on him when after many years of trying, counseling, working through tears, his first marriage ended in divorce. As Michael Card notes in his book *The Walk*, Lane with all his degrees, publications, and accomplishments couldn't get a job, as Lane would say, "even as a garbage man."[12] Ron Nash, chair of the department at WKU offered Lane a position which was initially part-time. A hard-nosed scholar with a gracious heart, Lane had a big booming voice that filled corridors. Card and his wife, Susan, though they had long since graduated, drove in from out of town to attend a couple of those New Testament Theology lectures.

Lane was not only an exact and brilliant scholar but also a gifted storyteller. He entertained us with the stories such as the one of the Harvard scholar A.D. Nock. The story, often retold, recounts the day when the world-renowned Pauline scholar, Professor Nock, was relaxing in his bachelor quarters at Harvard, reading the newspaper in the manner in which he was most comfortable, in his birthday suit. The maid entered and upon seeing him screamed, "Oh my God!" To which Nock quickly replied, "Oh no, no madam, just his humble servant."

Lane also shared with me one day the story of when he was at Harvard and the dean called him into his office and said, "Bill, you're a brilliant doctoral student about to graduate, and we can do so much to push your career. But there's just one problem. Your position on the inspiration of Scripture is too high." Lane replied, true to his deep faith, "I can do no other."

One of the requirements of Lane's class was that one kept a journal of one's interactions with the assigned readings. I wrote poetry, drank coffee, talked philosophy, listened to all the guest lecturers that came to campus, spent time in the library reading books that had nothing to do with my course work, went to movies, and this left hardly any time to read the assigned texts, or to work on all the papers which were required. Our parents' shadows find themselves in our lives in new and unexpected ways. Dad had

12. Card, *The Walk*, 11.

his own ways to court self-destruction and so did I. The other main way I engaged in such activities was through rapid acceleration. I didn't really understand what a problem I had until one-day no one in the family would loan me a vehicle citing a long catalogue of grievances: driving my brother's Jeep into a tree, the Datsun pickup into a fence, blowing the engines on the 63 Buick Riviera and my brother's motorcycle, and taking mom's Volkswagen Rabbit down a snow covered Ozark mountain. We are never as free from our ghosts as we pride ourselves.

Toward the end of the semester, we turned in our journals. After they were graded, he returned them. As he was passing them out, he said, "Mr. Gehring, I would like to see you in my office after class." I knew that was not good news. My journal of interactions with the New Testament Theology readings was entitled *Free-Wheeling with a Yamaha 650 named Ernie on Highway 22 while the Broken White Lines Become One*.

In the journal there were a few interactions with the assigned readings but there were also a lot of interactions with literature and contemporary culture: Pink Floyd's *The Wall*, lyrics from Don McLean, and quotes from Augustine, Dostoevsky, and a tip of the hat to Dietrich Bonhoeffer. Sprinkled into it, as well, were original poems and other compositions. When I entered into his floor to ceiling bookshelf lined office, Lane said, "Have a seat." I felt somewhat like a rebel facing the guillotine. He began, "This journal is so much less than what I expected." No news flash there, I thought. I've heard that song and dance a few times short of the number of sands on the seashore. That was not surprising but what he did next struck me dumb. He said, "But it is also so, so very much more than I ever expected." He continued with words of encouragement. He asked me if he could make a copy of it, and I said, "Sure." Not totally sure why he wanted a copy, but I felt it wasn't because he was short on paper for his Water Closet. But one never knows for sure. Years later I learned from him that at WKU and at other institutions where he taught, he read passages from the journal to his students.

Reading it now, it is somewhat odd for the fifty-seven-year-old me to meet the twenty-three-year-old I once was. In journal I explained the title:

> This is a rather long title, but perhaps it best captures my dream. An end to the fragmentation that I feel all around me, and unfortunately perceive within me. An end to fragmentation, the phrase alone produces a sweet taste as it rolls off the tongue. Yet it is not something I will see in this fallen world. Completeness,

wholeness, consummate, absolute, entire, fulfilled, accomplished, are all words that I will never completely understand until he who was in the beginning passes his sin pierced hand through my heart and restores the balance of my soul.

After more than three decades later, having lived through all the news reports and tragedies of our world, having seen so much brokenness, so much injustice, my heart's prayer remains much the same.

It was Lane, the one who experienced the church turning its back on him, who turned me back to the church. Lane challenged me to read the gospels and note, again and again, the emphasis on community. I did. We met in his office for further conversations. In time, I began to understand that there is no theistic individualism to be found there, just a broken, failing community that God calls to be witnesses to his grace. In response to his reframing my concept of church, I decided to apply to seminary. I didn't apply to seminary as one who looked forward to the journey. I applied in the spirit of Jonah of old: begrudgingly, reluctantly, and hurriedly (judging from all the spelling mistakes made in the seminary application). I applied to only one. It was the one reputed to have a serious endowment. I didn't investigate whether they had any decent faculty members or produced any significant scholars. That was not on my radar screen. My only criterion was that since I didn't have a clue how I was going to utilize this degree, I didn't want to incur any more than absolutely necessary debt. Everything had to work out just right or I would see that as validation that the collar didn't apply to me. Like tumblers in the lock, everything fell into place.

III. Elmer Gantry and a Geneva Gown

Having made the mistake of attending Evangel sight unseen, I knew I wouldn't repeat that blunder. After the semester at WKU ended, I traveled to the Princeton Theological Seminary to see what it was like. Walking around the campus, spending time in the library, strolling through the university and into downtown, I decided there were certainly worse places I could hang out for three years even if I were uncertain of the outcome. Heading back to Arkansas, I decided to matriculate at PTS in the fall. I just didn't know what I would do with the degree. But that was three years away. Enough time to struggle with theology, the faith, the church as institution, and the thorn in my side, the wound that wouldn't heal, theodicy.

I spent the summer working at the Trading Post and Mini Mall opening and closing the store, sometime running the cash register, and other times hauling out for customers' cases of Old Milwaukee, Budweiser, Miller, Moosehead, and all the other flavors the beer trucks brought to the store, loading them into beat up pickup trucks, Cadillacs, and every now and then a Mercedes or a BMW that had driven over from Russellville. Word had gotten out that I was going to seminary to some faraway place in the northeast and people I didn't know inquired, "What are you going to do with a degree like that?" I had no answer to give. Often, I would tell them that I was going to study theology because it was just too difficult to articulate that I was considering the ministry. Sometimes I found it too insurmountable to admit it even to myself, fearing that if I traveled that way somehow, I would morph into Elmer Gantry. I worried about that for years. One day, after I had graduated from seminary and was interviewing with a Board of Ordained Ministry, I verbalized this fear. Some salty, well-seasoned Methodist preacher, who had weathered far too many storms, said after my disclosure, "Don't worry kid. You ain't got it in you." He was saying in effect that I was too cerebral, too boring, and too afraid of emotion to ever be able to pull that off. I felt, in that moment, both reassured and offended, as if I were some kind of evangelistic underachiever who was incapable of winning crowds over with a winsome smile and a gregarious personality.

It is interesting to note that, at this time, for a great part of America, ministry was the second most trusted profession, second only to pharmacists. Thanks to the TV evangelists and the Roman Catholic hierarchy, ministry has fallen considerably in the trust poll. But in New Blaine, at that point in time more than three decades ago, people were working too hard to scrape by to appreciate why anyone would want to complete a degree that they were uncertain of its utility. The denizens of my hometown were, by and large, practical people. If one of their children went to university, they went for sensible skills like accounting, computer programming, or training to be a teacher or a nurse. New Blaine was heavily unchurched long before the demographic consultants started talking about the Nones. As summer came to a close, I made preparations for the next stage of the journey. Spending some time with my then eighty-five-year old Grandmother, I couldn't imagine the time when she wouldn't be there. Finally, the day arrived and my brother took me to the airport.

Like many Southerners before me, I quickly became infatuated with Princeton. The buildings were made of stone which seemed a good deal more permanent than Evangel's wooden barracks. History permeated the air. Taking long walks, I read every historical marker I came across. I went on a walking tour, and we took in the barracks, Nassau Hall, the university chapel, and the cemetery. Buried there were notables such as Archibald Alexander, Sylvia Beach, Aaron Burr, Grover Cleveland, Jonathan Edwards, Charles Hodge, B.B. Warfield, and John Witherspoon. But the one who towered out above the rest was the one who faced the south as his back was toward the university, Paul Tulane. Tulane offered what was then the College of New Jersey, later to be known as Princeton University, a great deal of money in exchange for naming the school after him; they refused. He found a school in New Orleans grateful for the piles of cash he provided and left a lasting monument to register his bitterness.

Princeton was a whole new world. I attended lectures of guest writers and scholars at the university, spent a great deal of time in Firestone Library reading everything but the assigned texts, drank a river of coffee in Chancellor Green, made trips to the Jersey coast, and took the Dinky to Princeton Junction and the train into New York City. I toured the MET, went to bookstores, bought records, and visited Lady Liberty, trying to visualize my Grandfather as a young man entering a new land. Weekday evenings were spent in the Annex where whisky sours were reasonable and theological talk of friends sustaining. Friday nights were at Italian restaurants in Chambersburg and Saturday mornings at PJ's Pancake House. I worked at Princeton Video Express on Nassau Street to have money enough to hang with my friends. They had more money, for the most part, than I had as some had denominational scholarships, grants, Rockefeller Theological Fellowships, and family monies. I spent just enough time writing papers and studying for exams so that I wouldn't be, like Adam of old, expelled from paradise.

IV. Three Questions

After becoming an associate pastor at a large Methodist church in Charlotte, NC, a few years after graduating from Seminary, I noticed something that I hadn't experienced in quite that same degree before. Upon meeting someone new, a fair number of Charlotteans would pepper the stranger with three questions: Where do you go to church? Where do you live? And where do you work? The inquirer was able to find out a good deal about someone from those seemingly innocuous questions. In fact, by answering these three questions, some people knew whether they wanted to get to know you better or not. I was able to answer all of those questions at that point in my life. One time, a soup kitchen worker directed me to feel the keys in my pocket; then he said, "Now that's what separates you from a great many of our clients. One of those keys will fit into an ignition of your car and drive you to a home where another key will open the door and you can lay down your head in relative safety and peace." Able to answer all three of those questions, I was one of the privileged with a parsonage, a steady income, a church to call home, and acceptable skin color. I never will forget a classmate sharing how he was stopped while riding his bicycle around Princeton because an officer thought somehow that he didn't belong, that he was an interloper from urban Trenton. His pain and anger began an opening of my eyes. In Charlotte, not only did I have a lovely parsonage in which to live but it was also at one of those prized addresses. The check-out clerks at the Harris Teeter remarked about it when I paid for the groceries with a check.

In seminary, no one asked where I worked, for we were all students, but they did want to know to which church I belonged. Their questions involved both the denomination and the particular local expression of it. Many of them were from large Presbyterian churches whose pastors had also attended Princeton Theological Seminary, large Presbyterian churches that the president of the seminary visited on his fund-raising tours. Disclosing that I grew up Roman Catholic, sojourned for a while with the uninhibited Pentecostals, and was currently unaffiliated, they looked relieved that I wouldn't be, three years down the road, competing for one of their jobs in the affluent world of the Presbyterian denomination. There were days when I thought that PTS was a bit of a finishing school preparing bright, young, descendants of doctors, lawyers, and CEO's to take their rightful places in Rotary Clubs and large steeple churches across the nation.

It wasn't long before one of my friends, one evening while drinking cheap Margaritas at Chi-Chi's on Route One, prophesied that someday I would start a new denomination called the First Church of Mikie. Everyone laughed and I responded, "Though it has a pleasant ring to it, I'm quite confident that it won't pay well." Of course, being too much a child of Rome, I could never travel into that hinterland of non-denominational Christianity creating an institution in my own image. Though having no problem ceasing church attendance a few years earlier, I never thought the answer was to be found in becoming the pope or bishop of my own church. I valued church history far too much for that. My appreciations not only of history but also of the liturgical traditions of the church are some of the reasons why I could never find it within myself to join an Assemblies of God church.

As the semester wore on, I began to envy my friends who had settled or had settled for them the denominational question. They enjoyed denominational scholarships, food packages from their home churches, and when their senior pastors visited the school, they were taken out for dinner. I started thinking about which denomination I would consider joining. The Presbyterians were ruled out for two reasons: first, John Calvin's role in Michael Servetus' execution seemed like flawed DNA, and second, since a great number of my friends were Presbyterian, I didn't want to follow the crowd. Lutheranism seemed like an obvious choice and it is hard not, on some level, to love Martin Luther.[13] Any man who marries a nun to spite the Pope captures my attention. There is so much to begrudge the Pope about but for some strange reason I didn't call Lutheranism home. In hindsight, it seems like it would have been a good fit. The Episcopal Church also seems like an obvious choice and Henry VIII's separation from Rome didn't surprise me greatly. Politicians do what politicians do, or as they say, "It's great to be king!" And if it weren't for the fourth edition of Williston Walker's *A History of the Christian Church* I probably would have joined the Episcopal Church.

After my Pentecostal sojourn, I no longer possessed an attraction to low-church denominations: Baptist, Church of Christ, etc. and I had long lumped the Methodists in that category. After all they were called the *shouting Methodists* and I had endured all the shouting I could possibly suffer through. Truth is though, lumping the Methodists in the category of the Low Church was a prejudice and I really didn't know anything about the Methodists. But in reading Walker's ever-so-dry and fact-filled book, I met John Wesley, the son of an Anglican priest who was plucked like a brand from a parsonage fire set by disgruntled parishioners. Not only did I like John Wesley immediately, I also liked his father, Samuel. It's not everyone who has the gift of getting his parishioners so agitated that they burn down the house in which you and your family live. Now that takes a real skill set.

13. Of course, there is plenty about Martin Luther that gives great offense, especially his abhorrent anti-Semitic views.

John's devotional life and faith formation was shaped more by his mother Susanna than anyone else. I learned how John went to Oxford and was deeply steeped not only in the high church but also in the theology and traditions of the early church. After graduating, he became a Fellow of Lincoln College and could have spent his days in the comfortable routine of the academic life in the wonderlands of Oxford, spending his days reading in the Bodleian Library, tutoring the not always open minds of the sons of landed gentry and aristocracy, perusing the bookshops, and having tea at any number of establishments, but not Wesley. A storm was brewing in him wrestling with what it means to live a disciplined Christian life and how should one spend one's life in service to God's kingdom. In time, Wesley and his brother Charles signed up to go to the new world so that they could minister to the colonists in Savannah and Fort Frederica. They also wanted to convert the Native Americans. As time passed in the new world, trouble developed, and Charles sailed back to England. John persevered. At Fort Frederica, Wesley demonstrated that an acorn doesn't fall far from the tree, and some of his parishioners were so angry at him that they filed legal proceedings against him. And no one, upon learning that he was leaving, attempted to persuade him to stay. That concluded Wesley's solo pastorate and never again would he subject himself to the expectations and demands of a congregation.

Wesley failed in his mission to America and sailed back to England, dejected, heart-broken, and worried about all the implications that leaving the new world with charges hanging above him might mean. In his journey to America, Wesley came in contact with the enthusiastic Moravians and he wanted to have the bold faith that they seemed to enjoy. Out of his failure, a spiritual rebirth transformed his life and his ministry. Failure takes us deeper into God; success is fought with temptations of apple-eating, thinking that we can be independent, and believing that the self-made creature no longer needs a Creator. Wesley's failure anchored his soul in God and from there he would live into the maxim that the world is his parish. After his Aldersgate experience, Wesley so developed the confidence and the heart for God's mission field that he engaged in outdoor preaching which was a practice that he, as an Oxford educated Anglican clergyman, considered most "vile." He endured his mission to share the gospel despite the various persecutions he suffered for his iterant preaching. Wesley, for the sake of the proclamation of the Gospel, refused to confine himself to society's expectations of how a divine should conduct himself and he unleashed a movement that would transform lives and communities.

During my senior year in high school, I read a biography on St. Francis that captivated my imagination; I was amazed by how he sought to bring renewal to the Roman Catholic Church and by how he didn't seek to break away from it. Wesley also tried, in a manner of speaking, to do the same. For more than half-a-century, the Methodist movement remained loosely related to the Anglican Church hoping to bring spiritual vitality to the Mother Church and by extension to all of England. It was a Eucharistic crisis which necessitated Wesley's dramatic actions. In America, the Methodist movement was growing far and wide as the frontier opened and there were no ordained preachers to give communion. The Anglican Church in America after the Revolution was being repackaged for a new country. But what would they have to do with each other anyway? It's almost like asking what does Athens have to do with Jerusalem? What would proper Anglicans now rebranded as Episcopalians make of the loud and rambunctious Methodists?

People needed the sacrament of grace and Wesley made a way. In 1784, he consecrated Thomas Coke, a fellow Oxford educated Anglican priest, as a superintendent to go to America and ordain the Methodist preachers so that they could consecrate the elements, so that the body of Christ could be lifted up, broken, and shared among the people. So that the cup of sacrifice, the wine, the blood of Christ, could be partaken of and lives changed.

What I discovered in John Wesley was someone who combined High Church Anglicanism with the enthusiasm of the Moravians, and that seemed to be an apt template to make sense of the spiritual journey of one who had been reared and educated in Benedictine monasticism (in conservative Roman Catholicism) and who had traveled for a season among the wild-eyed, God-loving, loud-shouting Pentecostals.

V. The Corner Crucifix

Upon deciding on Methodism, I closed my Church History textbook and picked up the phone calling a couple of friends, David and Michael. We walked to the Annex and toasted my new-found denomination. I didn't understand the irony of that. The following Sunday, they went with me to Princeton Methodist Church and there for the very first time I experienced a United Methodist Church service. It was great. The preacher was scholarly and the service liturgical. I figured that all United Methodist Churches would be like Princeton since John Wesley was, after all, an Oxford divine. After the service, we went back to the Seminary's cafeteria for lunch and I was ebullient. David turned to me and said, "You know they are called singing Methodists for a reason?" Puzzled, I replied, "Yeah." He then emphatically said, "You didn't sing a note in the entire service. Not once."

In time, the preacher at Princeton UMC put me in contact with George Morris who was looking for a seminarian to work in his church, and I found a very welcoming congregation at Trinity UMC in Ewing, NJ, which is right across the street from what was then called Trenton State University, now called the College of New Jersey. George, an incredible pastor, was an amazing mentor. I found a home at Trinity.

The denominational question was settled but still I was troubled by James' death. None of the arguments of attempting to keep God out of the dock on the problem of suffering resonated. None of the arguments seemed compelling enough to solve the age-old problem of pain. I felt about them much like that Oxford don in the English Department who upon considering C.S. Lewis's first direct-apologetic book said, "The problem of pain is quite bad enough without Lewis making it worse."[14]

One night during my first year in Seminary, I had a dream. Years before I had abandoned recording my dreams or attributing any significance to them. Sipping at the waters of modernism had affected me. Dreams now were things that occurred when drinking too many Rolling Rocks and eating far too many slices of cheap, greasy, pepperoni pizza. But this dream was different. In it my nephew James who looked the same had a conversation with me. It's been more than three decades now and I don't remember the content of the conversation except what he told me at the end but I do remember how vibrant, intelligent he was, noting his increased vocabulary, and how he almost sparkled. And then he said to me, "Don't worry Uncle Mike. It's all alright. I'm good. Don't worry about me anymore."

Now I can't say with empirical certainty that this dream was definitely from God. Of course not, and there's a great many things that I put my full weight upon which lack empirical certainty. But what I can say is that the next morning I had a peace which had eluded me for several years. Looking over to the corner of my room, I beheld the crucifix and remembered how God co-suffers with us and how mystery is a component of the faith. How God experienced death on Good Friday and understands our pains and

14. Wilson, *C.S. Lewis*, 181.

agonies. I remembered how crucifixion Friday was followed by Silent Saturday that gave way to Resurrection Sunday and how, in that moment, God spoke a resounding "yes" to the world's "no." It's not that my heart stopped aching for James. It still aches for him as it does, as well, for my niece Carolyn who died before her time. The ache will continue until time itself fades into eternity. But the hope I carry, as a believer, sees me through the fog of this world and through some of the almost impenetrable mysteries of the faith. This hope sustains me even when I'm seeing through a glass darkly.

VI. Theological Transitions

Before arriving at Seminary, I already had some familiarity with the various kinds of biblical criticisms: textual, literary, tradition, historical, form, and redaction. Some of my classmates had not been exposed to it and seemed shell-shocked when in *Introduction to Old Testament* the professors started dissecting the texts like surgeons on amphetamines. It was not surprising when an evangelical backlash arose from the students who came to faith through the work of *Young Life* or some other student outreach ministry. After a few weeks, they settled into the grove and became acclimatized. The professors could have been more attuned to the reality that in every lecture they were lobbying grenades into edifices of faith that were constructed of various materials. Some students came with an undergraduate in religious studies and seemed solid like stone. Others were recent converts filled with excitement letting the Spirit blow through them like they were open-flap tents. Some appeared solid like wood, raised in the church, having been taught by a long-line of revered Sunday School teachers, only to have it all burn down into a pile of ash. And the phoenix, in those burned-out souls, doesn't always rise. This was in the days before seminaries started to pay attention to spiritual formation. Back then, our education focused on academically mastering the materials. Students dealt with the cognitive dissonance in various ways.

One of the great epistemological Trojan horses of unbelief is inerrancy.[15] It seemed that the students who suffered the greatest faith losses were

15. The Apostle Paul taught that all Scripture is inspired by God and useful for teaching. (2 Timothy 3:16) The difficulty of attributing the word "inerrant" to the Scriptures is that, in the minds of some, the popular denotation of the word inerrant is without error. Without error means different things to different people and some biblical scholars have demonstrated creative ways of dancing around in a herculean effort to maintain inerrancy despite the inconsistencies found in Scripture. Since not all who are raised in

those from conservative fundamentalist churches. Their churches didn't prepare them for the variety of interpretations present in the academy. I had been taught, as a child, by a parish priest, that the faith contains a great deal of mystery. I had been raised to believe that when the host was held high and the bell rang that it literally became the body of Christ, corpuscles, and all. When one has been brought up in such a belief system, the differences between how Matthew, Mark, and Luke told the story was not that problematic. I was just glad that they took the time to tell the story and didn't get side tracked by *Hogan's Heroes*, dancing mistresses, or any of the other distractions that the world offers. Furthermore, I expected there to be differences. God did not create us to be robots. Nor was I bothered that John was altogether different. I wasn't too worried about whether David killed Goliath or someone else did. I was just glad that the good guys won. I would have preferred that Goliath didn't have to die, that he found Jesus and became a missionary to the brutes, or to the WWE (World Wrestling Entertainment), but things don't always work out that way for more reasons than just that he lived a thousand years before Christ. Sometimes in this old, broken, world of ours, every story doesn't end glad-fully.

I was also not greatly bothered by the miracle stories of whether it was possible or not for an axe head to float or for dead people to come back to life. It didn't trouble me that an oil pot never ran dry or that water was turned into wine. I wasn't bothered by any of those because I actually believed something far more audacious, something that would require a great deal more energy, and something that would make the previously

---

fundamentalist traditions possess the nuances of these biblical scholars, it is not too difficult to see how quickly existential faith crises can develop when reading the Scriptures. Any freshman undergraduate studying the different accounts of the Resurrection narratives quickly discovers that the writers possessed a different sense of recounting events than their university professor. The problem of inerrancy is not a problem of whether orthodox Christians believe that all Scripture is inspired by God and useful for teaching. Of course, orthodox Christians believe that. The difficulty of inerrancy is found in applying a twenty-first century denotation and connotation of the word to a first-century text. When individuals who are raised in faith traditions which drum in inerrancy discover the inconsistencies in Scripture, their house of faith too easily can become a house of cards. All of this is unnecessary. Inerrancy is a quest for authority and power not unlike papal infallibility. Both came to exert greater prominence in the midst of the western cultural wars of the eighteenth, nineteenth, and twentieth centuries. As capitalism, communism, socialism, humanism, scientism threatened traditional church authority, some traditions found ways to re-exert their authority. One of the evangelistic intentions of the Gospel writers was not just to record their historical observations and theology about Jesus but to introduce the reader to the living Lord of the Resurrection.

mentioned look like cheap magician tricks. I profess that God created everything out of nothing. I prefer to express it that God spoke it into being or like in *The Magician's Nephew* sang it into being. The cosmologists worry about how it happened and when it happened, but I'm convinced I know who made it happen.

What I did notice about the miracles in the Gospel is that even with them, there was a lot of capriciousness present and left unexplained. For example, why was only one person healed that day when Jesus stopped at the pool of five porticoes (Bethzatha)?[16] He enters the place that has a reputation that when an angel of the Lord stirs the water the first one in will be healed. At this pool, surrounded by so many invalids—lame, blind, paralyzed—all there waiting, praying, desperate for their miracle, Jesus heals only one. Can you imagine their souls being stirred into a torrent as they witnessed someone healed besides them? Don't you just wonder if they cried out, "Hey Jesus, what about me?" I'm sure some thought that if Jesus didn't remember them then they weren't going to remember him. One wonders, in the Jerusalem crowd that cried out for Barabbas, those who cried out for Jesus' crucifixion, if any of them were made bitter by their failure to get a miracle. Even in the text, mystery roams across the landscape so much so that it ought to be personified with a character.

Though entering Seminary with a religion undergraduate major, I was still affected. The theologian who resonated most (in addition to John Wesley) was Karl Barth, the Swiss pastor with strong socialist leanings who in the crisis of the First World War rose up against the moral and theological bankruptcy of liberal Protestantism.[17] Barth fed my soul, but the readings in his theological opponent wearied my spirit. Though Rudolf Bultmann impacted me, I never bought into his project.[18] Unlike him, I had no prob-

---

16. Some refer to it as Bethesda and others Bethsaida; see John 5:2–9.

17. Karl Barth (1886–1968), a German-Swiss theologian, served as pastor of the working-class reformed congregation in Safenwil, Switzerland from 1911–1921. He then went on to teach in the universities at Göttingen, Münster, Bonn and Basel. Though trained in Liberal Protestantism, Barth reacted against that tradition when his saw that some of his former professors signed *The Manifesto of Ninety–three German Intellectuals to the Civilized World*, a document that supported the Kaiser's war ambitions. While still in Safenwil, Barth wrote a commentary on the Epistle to the Romans. Though he himself did not appreciate the term, Barth is considered a leading proponent of Neo-Orthodoxy.

18. Rudolf Bultmann (1884–1976) was one of the leading New Testament theologians of the twentieth century. He spent the great majority of his teaching career at the University of Marburg. Bultmann believed that the Scriptures need to be demythologized from its primitive mythological world-view in order to make the Bible relevant to

lem believing in the spirit and wonder world of the New Testament and still availing myself of electricity and modern medicine. But yet deep down, a sense of loss was in all of it. Though never giving up belief in the Nicene Creed, there were times that it felt like a trumpet call from a far distant country, echoing and almost muted, like a love song that one could hardly even remember its words.

Yet with all the flickering and dark nights of the soul, the words were there, buried deep, ready to be found new all over again.

VII. Homeward Bound

It was March of my last semester at Princeton, and I knew full well that even Adam had to leave Eden. Graduation approached and I had two alternatives in my mind. My senior thesis was on F.W.J. Schelling's *System of Transcendental Idealism*. Schelling, a German Idealist philosopher, who was friends and competitor with G.W.F. Hegel, wrote his philosophical treatise at the age of twenty-five and attempted to systematize all of reality, and the key to understanding it is found in aesthetic intuition. To this day, I have no clue why I spent two semesters reading this murky-headed German but, at the time, I found his thought captivating. My supervising professor wrote to the University of St. Andrews about the prospects of me studying there.

The second option was to start a house painting business. In the summers, I worked for A-1 Painting Company making the houses in Princeton and the surrounding communities look fresh and clean. My plan was to start a painting business in Newport, Rhode Island. The salt water ensures a constant supply of work, and I had a free place to live. Since I wouldn't have to pay for rent, a great amount of what I earned could be poured back into a business and hopefully before long I could have two crews, then three, etc. A professor, Charlie, owned a house in Middletown. His nephew lived in the house, and he was frustrated with his nephew's lack of direction. Charlie believed that I would be a good influence on him. Bruce, a Deadhead, seemed to work only enough to gather together monies to travel the country in his Volkswagen bus following the Grateful Dead from venue to venue. Bruce was a great guy and his girlfriend was also a Deadhead, which meant that there would be long periods of time when I would be the only one in the house. It seemed like the best plan as I really didn't believe a PhD from St. Andrews would lead to employment. Even in the eighties,

---

the modern person.

the university world, with respect to religious studies, was glutted. Further-more, I had no money, and I wasn't going to take loans to study overseas.

Though fairly content with my plan, yet one day, somewhere around the middle of March, skipping class, staring at the ceiling of the dorm room in Brown Hall, I pondered my future. Why pursue a degree that I might not use? Hanging out in the bars of Newport would provide ample opportunity to drop a line here or there about the competing positions on the dating of the Gospel of John, but was that going to be the sole use of these three years of study ending up as a theological Cliff Clavin from the TV show *Cheers*? Looking to the floor, I noticed a book. It was *And Are We Yet Alive?* by Richard Wilke, the United Methodist Bishop of Arkansas. We had to read the book for one of the Methodism courses. Even though my plan for Rhode Island seemed like a great idea, I felt perplexed that I would be graduating with a Master of Divinity having never served a full-time ap-pointment in the church. I felt conflicted by the old hounds from my past, from my childhood and teenage years, afraid that they weren't going to leave me alone until finally I relented. Perhaps a phone call would seal the deal. If I made the call and the Bishop seemed uninterested (and why would he be interested, for heaven's sake, given my discursive spiritual journey) then that would be that; Newport here I come, living large and loud with a clear conscience and a total sense of being released, free.

Calling information for the number for the Bishop's office in Little Rock, I wrote it down and dialed. My heart felt like it was going to knock down the walls of my chest. "The Bishop's office," the receptionist cheerfully said. "Yes, I'm a seminary student and I would like to speak with Bishop Wilke." She put me right through. I'm sure it must have been one of the strangest calls the Bishop received that day or probably in the course of his bishopric days. I began in a rambling way. "Hello, Bishop Wilke, my name is Michael Gehring and I'm about to graduate with a Master of Divinity from Princeton Theological Seminary and I don't know hardly any Methodists in Arkansas even though I'm from Arkansas. I was raised Roman Catholic, and I joined a Methodist Church in New Jersey." His first response to me was, "Well I'm a Yale man myself," and the conversation flowed. He seemed to have no one else he needed to talk to that day for he spent all the time in the world with me. Sharing with him that I was debating about attending St. Andrews, I also disclosed that I might want to serve a church. We ended the call with a commitment to stay in touch.

Sometime after that I let him know that I decided to postpone St. Andrews for a few years. I did not let him know about the house painting business plan. On March 21, he sent me a letter letting me know that they needed me in Arkansas, which made me think that they must not have had a bumper crop of candidates that year. He told me that I needed to talk to my pastor and get approved as a candidate for ordained ministry. Trinity had the Charge Conference on April 20. I was assigned a mentor and had to work through the Candidacy Guide Book and then appear before the District Committee of the Southern New Jersey Board of Ordained Ministry. While all that was going on, I flew to Arkansas to meet the Bishop and interview before a committee that he had gathered. They sweet tea-ed and dined me. After the interview, the meal, the flattery, I departed that Friday evening for the family farm a couple of hours from Little Rock. On Sunday morning, I received a phone call that I had been appointed to a church and that I would begin the first week of July.

May came and went. Everything was a bit of a blur with finals, papers, and wrapping up the last three years of my life. As I prepared to move back to Arkansas, I was mournful that I was leaving Princeton. Princeton is not a great place for everyone. It's no accident that the door to the Graduate Tower of the University is kept locked. But for me, someone who was never driven academically, who never took grades too seriously, who slept through far too many classes, cut others for no good reason, and researched and wrote papers in the wee morning hours before they were due, someone who allowed his senior thesis on German Idealism to continually be interrupted by *Hogan's Heroes,* Princeton was the closest place to paradise I have ever encountered. It was in Princeton that I took a beautiful student (Rhonda) from Westminster Choir College to drink hot tea, late one winter's evening, in the courtyard of the Institute for Advanced Study, while the moon lit up the night. The stars must have aligned themselves for later she, a native of the borderlands of the Carolinas, followed me to what was once known as the last-stop of civilization before entering the dangerous territories.

Chapter Four

Inhabiting

I. Reichsbischof Müller, Liberation Theology, and the American Dream

THOUGH I'VE HAD MANY parishioners inquire about what it was like to go from Roman Catholicism to United Methodism, I have not experienced anyone asking what it was like to inhabit United Methodism. Obviously, a significant number of people I interact with are Methodists and some of them have a tendency to believe that Methodism occupies the high ground. A few of them have actually asked, "Why would anyone want to be anything other than United Methodists?" I have listened to clergy and laity wax eloquently about their great-grandfathers and great-great-grandfathers who were Methodist circuit riders, riding on their horses with little desks mounted on them so that they could work on their Greek, theology, and sermons as they bounced along the dirt roads.

In my office are statues of four popes: Pope John Paul II that my mother bought at the Vatican, Pope Ratzinger that my son and I acquired while we were following in the footsteps of St. Paul, Pope Francis, a gift from Rhonda and the children one Christmas and it waves when the sunshine hits it, and lastly one of Pope John Wesley. Early Methodism, some say, didn't have a great problem with authority since Holy Father John Wesley made the critical decisions for the movement. Protestantism's Achilles heel, the problem of authority (and in other ways its strength) has been a difficulty from its beginnings. Jeffrey Stout, an ethicist at Princeton University, noted that individuals and societies have long been in a flight from authority.

If one disregards papal infallibility and *sola scriptura*, then what is a religious community's criterion for truth? *Sola scriptura*, though it sounds rather august, crumbles in upon itself. It is painfully clear for any observer that there are a variety of teachings represented in the Old and New Testaments and some are in conflict with others. Who will be the community's or denomination's spokesperson to determine which scriptures are privileged over others? *Sola scriptura* makes a cool battle cry, but in actuality it is conceptually difficult. Who will serve as the official hermeneutical agent and truth interpreter? Due to this problem of authority within Protestantism, ideological conflicts become like raging forest fires that devour everything it is path.

In conversations about authority in the church, one hears United Methodists invoke the Wesley Quadrilateral, which holds that there are four sources for church doctrine: Scripture, tradition, reason, and experience. United Methodists contend that of the four, Scripture is primary (*prima scriptura*). However, such a well-thought out position as that still has not solved the problem of authority within United Methodism. Because there is not one single voice and because there is not presently within the United Methodist Church a universal agreement to abide by conciliar decrees (i.e. the General Conference's decisions) or to be actually governed by *the Book of Discipline*, conflicts boil over and never seem to be resolved. To an outsider, United Methodism must, at times, appear to be a deeply conflicted community intent on devouring itself.

What has it been like for me, as one who was raised in Roman Catholicism to pitch my tent within United Methodism? The UMC, as I write this, is in the midst of the greatest constitutional crisis that it has experienced since its founding in 1968. It is also the greatest crisis of its founding member denominations since the Methodist Episcopal Church in 1844 split into two denominations, northern and southern, over the issue of slavery. An interesting historical note is that at one point the southern church adopted as its official name: The Methodist Episcopal Church in the Confederate States of America. As painful as it is to admit that not only lay Methodists owned slaves but even a Methodist bishop (James Osgood Andrew). The southern Methodist church traveled a long way from John Wesley who staunchly opposed the slave trade. Wesley would have raged against how the southern Methodists were so at ease in Zion and so at ease, as well, with their accommodation to a great social evil.

The issue which threatens the unity of the United Methodist Church is a different kind of struggle, but it also is one of great angst as the church grapples to understand where the lines of inclusion versus exclusion are. Before I turn my attention to the current crisis of the UMC, before I consider United Methodism at the crossroads, permit me to go back in time and bring the story forward.

I joined the United Methodist Church because I resonated with John Wesley. What I did not give due consideration to was Wesley's denominational heirs. Why did I join the United Methodist Church and not the Free Methodist Church, or the Wesleyan Church, or the Church of the Nazarene? The answer, which reflects a total lack of consideration of denominational politics, structure, or ideological conflicts, resides in the old political and business maxim: everything is local. Not having a car my first year in Princeton meant that my chief transportation was either by foot or by the Princeton Dinky, which took me to a bigger world. Princeton United Methodist Church was within walking distance.

Though I read books in seminary about Methodist structure, it was all theoretical. Furthermore, greatly affected by Gerald Moede and the vision of the Consultation on Church Union, I longed for reconciliation among the scattered protestant tribes.[1] It seemed self-evident that the existence of the many varieties of denominations reflected humanity's brokenness and inability to live in harmony with one another. The church preaches a heavenly message of goodwill, love for all, and peace on earth but engages in hand-to-hand combat over any number of theological and sociological issues. I learned in Seminary to be wary of the overly ideological whether the leanings are left or right. What I experienced from and found within myself, is that driven by dogma sometimes one is tempted to caricature those who question one's assumptions, and sometimes one is tempted to put value upon others based upon ideological alignment. In other words, relationships are, at times, sacrificed on the idol's altar of whatever ideology is of the moment. I had already lived through that with the right-leaning

1. The Consultation on Church Union (COCU) was founded in 1960. It sought to bring about dialogue and eventually, hopefully, prayerfully, the union of the member denominations. The conversation lasted for forty years but, in time, the reality became all too apparent that the union of member denominations was not going to happen, that such union would remain a dream rather than a reality. Gerald Moede served for fourteen years as the General Secretary of COCU.

Assemblies of God and now I experienced that not only with those on the opposite end of the spectrum, but also those who hold to the middle.

When I was in seminary, one of the raging issues was liberation theology which, of course, is greatly indebted to Marxist theory. As one who had traveled through Czechoslovakia and East Germany, the temptation to bite of that paradisiacal fruit was not overwhelming. When one questioned how it functioned in the economic world, one was, at times, labeled a right-wing fascist. Like C.S. Lewis, I don't care for fascists. Nor do I trust the collective which disregards the individual. After all, it was the High Priest who proclaimed that it was better for one man to die than the nation. It was better for Jesus to suffer on the cross and die a miserable death than to face the political unrest and Roman wrath. What I became accustomed to in seminary was that a whole lot of people talked high octane about matters that they, in fact, knew very little about. Tempted to sit silently rather than face the punitive nature of their judgment, more times than not, I waded deep into the waters of my own ignorance.

Any form of social-tinkering has unintended consequences. The Temperance Movement, whole-heartedly supported by the Methodist Church, fought a valiant fight and achieved a greater advancement than they ever could have hoped for as they successfully led the campaign, which resulted in banning of the production and sale of alcohol for approximately thirteen years in the United States. And one is hard-pressed not to admit the damage that alcohol inflicted and inflicts on many families with broken marriages, gambling losses, senseless acts of violence and, of course, forgetting where one has left one's children. Yet one also has to acknowledge that Prohibition gave rise to the rapid growth of organized crime. When the church engages politically it needs to do so with humility. Too often seminary conversations about social evils were more attuned to the prophet coming down the mountain with the law carved in stone. It was always more of a political charge than a systematic examination. It was a new form of Gnosticism that those who were the rightly initiated looked down upon those standing outside.

Reinhold Niebuhr spoke to my soul in a way that the liberation theologians never could. As a liberal-democrat, I strongly believed and believe that government, ideology, and new-found-crusades, all need checks and balances. As Paul wrote, we see through a glass darkly; now, we only know in part. In God's kingdom, all will be made right, but in the here and now someone is always scheming to gain power over others and will deploy whatever tools necessary, whether it is high flying rhetoric or coercive force, to manipulate others in their quest to be over-comers. The communist revolution seemed like a bright shiny dream worth giving one's life to, but now we know that hundreds of thousands of Russian Orthodox clergy, bishops, and nuns were murdered during Stalin's reign and the reign of other Soviet leaders. It is also estimated that millions of ordinary orthodox lay Christians were killed as well.

The readings in the German Church struggle greatly helped as they formalized, in my mind, that clergy should advocate the issues but not become attached to politicians or any nationalistic idols. Reichsbischof Ludwig Müller preaching a message of "Christ the Aryan" demonstrated just how easy the mixture of politics and religion can become a poisonous, toxic brew.[2] Müller, a Nazi, blinded by his ideology, allowed the Gestapo to spy on Lutheran churches. Blinded by his ideology, he endorsed murderous thugs. Political ideology, unencumbered by the ontological truth that every person is a child of God and has innate dignity and worth, becomes a seductress, leading individuals into places that they never thought possible. It induces people to forget that the primary claim upon their lives is God's kingdom.

I'm grateful that democracies have within them significant structural checks and balances to guard against the strong, charismatic leader who markets himself or herself as the one who has all the answers or more precisely claims to embody what is right as a tonic against the nation's ills. Democracies are fragile and dictators, whether they are benevolent or not, continually seek to undermine the various branches of government to maximize their political agendas. The church and preachers should advocate for the ancient messages of justice, mercy, and compassion for all whether they are descendants of those who settled the land centuries ago or whether they are brand new immigrants filled with the hopes and dreams that Lady Liberty so often inspires. When my Grandfather immigrated to the United States, it was against the backdrop of the escalating conflict in Europe, which led to the American involvement in the First World War. He, and many other German immigrants of that time, faced a wave of anti-immigrant, anti-German hostility. Lady Liberty is the ideal lived out in the

---

2. Ludwig Müller, a Lutheran pastor, served as a Navy Chaplain during the First World War. During the 1920's, he became associated with Nazism and eventually joined the party. He supported the purification of Christianity from its Jewish associations. In 1933, the Nazi government appointed him as Reichsbischof of the German Evangelical Church. He committed suicide after the Second World War ended.

reality of human fears, irrationalities, prejudices, and brokenness. Too often the church succumbs to the fear of others, fear of strangers, and fear of refugees but, as Will Willimon rightly noted, our faith calls us to overcome that and to meet the other in the person of Christ.[3]

Though seminary gave knowledge about how the church struggled through various Caesars, dictators, thugs, and villains, what I did not get enough of was practical skills in navigating the patriotism soon to be unleashed in congregations due to the first Gulf War, 9/11, Gulf War II, and all the other military engagements. Even the most patriotic has to admit that this country seems propelled to go from one war to another. This nation appears far too at ease spending its great treasury on war. I was not properly equipped to referee the heated discussions, which seems odd to say since I had already endured and participated in many ideological sparring endeavors.

What I did not realize as I headed into my first full-time appointment was how much the political conversations of seminary had in common with the political conversations of the church, not in terms of a particular brand of ideology, but in regards to how divisive they could be, how desperately short of the facts they often were, and how problematic the disagreements were in running institutions in an already conflicted society. Christ calls us into communion yet, so often, the body of Christ, both on the local level and the national level, is diverted from focusing on mission by seemingly never-ending conflicts. Christ calls us into union but too often the battles in the church become deeply personal and acrimonious.

When I began in the ministry, United Methodism was embroiled in a deep long-term struggle that had gone on for many years between the conservatives and the liberals. The flashpoints in this theological war ran the gamut from the flag in the sanctuary, to the proper interpretation of the inspiration of scriptures, to whether world-service dollars were being channeled into left-wing groups, etc. Though there were many divisive issues, the one that seemed to create the most heat, anger, passion, was the issue of homosexuality. On one-side stands the Good News Movement fighting to preserve the stance of *the Book of Discipline* and on the other, the Reconciling Network, attempting to bring about change. One of the tragic elements of this long-term struggle is people tend to put each other

---

3. Willimon, *Fear of the Other*, 89, 90. Will Willimon, retired United Methodist Bishop of the North Alabama Conference, is Professor of the Practice of Christian Ministry at Duke University.

into boxes. Classifications are drawn up, and people want to know whether you are in their camp or whether you are one of those. And those who try to inhabit the middle often times feel like a ping-pong ball. The "us versus them" is no way to mirror the self-emptying love of Christ.

As I began my first full-time appointment, I had no clue that one day, when I would be the age that I currently am with retirement on the horizon, the church would be in a greater mess than it was when I started. I had no clue that after three decades it would be more fragile, embroiled in deeper conflict, and accelerating its decline in worship attendance, members, and finances, but more about that later.

II. Five-Star Churches

With Princeton in my rear-view mirror, I headed out on the long-drive home. Breaking up the trip, I spent the night with Bill and Brenda Lane in Bowling Green. It was wonderful to see them again and to hear about Bill's writing projects. Hebrews was occupying his time. He asked about how I changed in Seminary, which professors made the greatest impact, and what are my thoughts about entering the pastorate. I did my best to answer, but I wasn't quite sure I knew myself. The next day, I journeyed on reaching the farm by night fall.

Before I knew it, time had passed like it had digested a mega-dose of caffeine pills. Not only had I already moved into the parsonage but now it was Saturday night and I awaited my first sermon with trepidation. I pondered whether I made a good decision or not to return home. No matter if the Asheville native, Thomas Wolfe, is ultimately right or wrong, returning home is never easy. There are ghosts to confront, decisions to second-guess, and an inward knot that won't untie. Feeling the collar close around my neck, fretting impending Sunday, I regretted the potential loss of freedom. Newport would have been nice: the salt-water breeze, fresh seafood, gilded mansions, and sidewalks with Gatsby wannabes hidden among the tourists.

Sitting in that small white frame parsonage, which seemed spacious after living for so long in a dorm room, I wondered, what could I possibly say the next day? It was the first but certainly not the last Saturday evening spent praying for a miracle: "Speak to me Lord; Speak to me now. You were with Moses on that cloudy mountain top; don't abandon me in this kairos of need." Having not been raised in a preaching tradition, I grappled how to make the message relevant. Through the years I've been amazed at children of Methodist clergy who themselves have gone on to become clergy and marveled at how easy this process came to them. Not me; my homiletical lottery awarded me the local priest reading a dull bishop's letter.

Karl Barth once said that we should hold the Bible in one hand and the newspaper in the other, but for a culture that had already traveled far too long down the road of entertainment perhaps the updated motto should have then been "one should hold the Bible in one hand and the TV guide in the other." (Now the motto would be to hold the iPhone, infinity of information and entertainment, in the palm of one's hand.) One parishioner, a FOB (Friend of Bill Clinton), who owned a successful business empire was so concerned when he heard that I didn't own a TV that he had one delivered without even asking if I wanted it or not. He definitely would have belonged to the Barth's school of Biblical interpretation as he wanted sermons to wrestle with the current news topics, but he would not have cared for Barth's politics. He was also the parishioner who rented billboards on I-40 which began with "While the behemoth sleeps. . ." They were anti-immigration billboards in the late eighties. The folks in the community where I came from, as they traveled up and down I-40, probably spent more time pondering the word "behemoth" than the proposed social policy.

My preaching anxiety certainly wasn't lessened by the knowledge of just how homiletically inexperienced I was. Before arriving at Cavanaugh, I had only preached two sermons in my life, both of them under protest. I would have had no clue how to go about that task if the request made my first year in Seminary had been granted. Marching one day into the office of one of the seminary's administrators, I informed her, in no uncertain terms, that I shouldn't be forced into taking two courses in speech and two courses in preaching since I had no desire whatsoever to go into the parish. I told her that I was in seminary only because I felt led to, and I wasn't overly thrilled about it, proclaiming that I was a Jonah surrounded not by water but by an endless sea of Presbyterian pastor wannabes. Sharing with her that I had been raised Roman Catholic, I emphasized that I didn't want to end up some crazy Protestant preacher, and that it would be a grave injustice to strong-arm me into taking courses that would prepare me for that which I don't want to be. "It was a justice issue," I stated resolutely. In a very maternal, nurturing and kind voice, this middle-aged Presbyterian clergy woman said, "Now, now, you poor dear, you shouldn't have to be forced to take all those speech and preaching classes." My spirits rallied; I breathed a sigh of relief and relaxed. Then her voice suddenly changed to a tone that would have made Margaret Thatcher shake in her boots, "But if you want a degree from Princeton Theological Seminary, you will take PR 01, PR 02, SP 01, and SP 02. Are we clear?" I quickly retreated from her office realizing that a vocational whale would be chomping me in half before I'd ever enter back into that foreboding space.

I had successfully avoided preaching during my first year of Field Education. In the second year, George, the Senior Pastor at Trinity UMC in Ewing, NJ, didn't even ask me if I wanted to preach. One Sunday, he simply stood before the congregation and said, "I've asked you all to sign-up for nursery duty. Since you all have not adequately signed-up, next Sunday I will be staffing the nursery and Mike will be preaching." My eyes must have almost popped out of my head based upon what parishioners reported to me after the service. The week after I preached my sermon, the secretary smiled as she shared that a good number of people immediately signed up for the nursery.

Now that I was entering the parish, I was grateful for that no non-sense seminary administrator. The parishioners were gracious and patient with their young preacher even when I appeared on that first Sunday wearing a white alb with a rope around my waist. Some murmured that their young preacher looked like a "damn Catholic."

The marching order I was given by the District Superintendent after I had arrived was to acquire a new parsonage. What I didn't know when I was appointed is that about two or three months before my meeting in April with the Bishop, Cavanaugh pitched a "royal fit" over the North Arkansas Conference's starting a new church development in Fianna Hills subdivision. The new church plant, St. Andrews, was given a bright, energetic young minister and Cavanaugh wanted to know why they were always given preachers close to retirement age. Some of the ladies who were especially displeased with the current pastor over the Fair Booth incident (which I will share shortly) got on the phone and started dialing. Never underestimate the power of retired ladies and their telephones. Cavanaugh, full of righteous indignation, demanded that the Bishop appoint them a young, energetic, seminary trained pastor. The District Superintendent tried his best. He brought one potential young minister right out of Emory University to tour the church, but his wife, upon seeing the parsonage said, "No." The DS, I suspect, worried for a while until the Bishop told him about a phone call from a young single seminarian about to graduate from a school in the northeast. He thought, "Well, he'll do."

After I had moved into the parsonage, it wasn't long before I started hearing about the great division within the congregation. No, it wasn't about homosexuality. You wouldn't have found many supporters within Cavanaugh for same-sex marriage back then. In fact, Cavanaugh, not too surprising, had strong cultural and political right leanings which, thanks to mom, I somewhat had a clue how to navigate. Mom had a massive oil painting of Ronald Reagan, *The Summit*, hanging in her home. It's a good thing Nancy kept a tight leash on him because if mom ever had a shot, she would have tried to lure him away. Though I'm a progressive Democrat, I've always been grateful that mom taught me the language and values of the cultural right as the majority of parishioners over the years have been cultural right and cultural middle.

Clergy have a difficult job of dealing with these conversations which can become overly heated quickly. Sometimes it's like threading the eye of a miniature needle attempting to influence parishioners to remember the traditional teachings of the church about social-justice while politicians inflame the base in order to get elected. Methodist DNA combines a message that advocates for the liberation of people from social captivity and injustice with personal transformation. The DNA is there even if, at various times in its history, as already mentioned, Methodism chose to operate as if it weren't. In the 1960's, Methodism was on the forefront of the civil rights struggle. I never will forget when a Buddha looking, scotch drinking, liberal Episcopalian New England professor said, "Thank God for the Methodists." Puzzled, I inquired why and he said, "If it weren't for them, the South would have gone totally Southern Baptist. My denomination was too weak to have a significant influence." Methodism does have, in comparison to some denominations, a powerful witness for social justice.

In the midst of all the ideological conflict, clergy have to work against the temptation to overpower others with one's own ideology, and this has been a struggle for me through the years. The end result of that conceptual move leads to the congregants check-mating the clergy person, totally shutting down receptivity. The raging storm at Cavanaugh wasn't about the economic injustice of the American capitalistic system, nor was it about our frequent military deployments. The conflict which created a deep divide concerned the Church's Fair Booth at the Arkansas-Oklahoma State Fair, which occurred toward the end of September and lasted a little over a week.

The church was renowned for its hot apple dumplings. For years and years, two ladies had run the fair booth (Nora and Nellie) as an act of service for the church. They would recruit the various workers, organize the whole thing, and at the end of it, give the church a nice big check to help with its budget. Some within the church started questioning whether it would be better for it to be a church-wide function rather than the domain of two ladies. Some murmured about the need for stricter financial controls. Upon getting to know them, I gave no credence to that gossip. The preacher who I followed aligned himself with the side that wanted change which, de facto, meant that he became a punching bag for those who were Nora/Nellie loyalists. It was then that I began to contemplate the wisdom of Switzerland. The ladies were hurt by power struggle, but the side that wanted the change prevailed. Nora and Nellie swore that they would have nothing else to do with it.

Many parishioners were happy to leave it to them because they didn't want to have to go to work at the Fair. I tried to coax the ladies back but failed. Fortunately, a parishioner named Harold stepped forward to coordinate the Fair Booth and, as you can guess, those who demanded the change really didn't want to be burdened with the responsibility of running it. I absolutely loved the fair booth. Making hamburgers, waiting on customers, and standing outside the booth hawking hot apple dumplings like a carnival barker was great fun. We sold a bunch of those apple dumplings.

One conversation stands out from those days. I'm working in the Fair Booth with a couple of folks, one of whom was Rayna. We were talking small talk when Rayna flat-out said, "I'm done with Billy Graham." Remember this is Arkansas, 1988, and that statement was equivalent to stopping the planet from spinning. Startled, I asked, "Why?" She said, "While watching him on TV last night, I saw that he read his prayer from a card. And I figured that if a man of the cloth can't say a prayer to the good Lord from his heart then he's no preacher that I want to listen to." Shocked, I replied, "But Rayna, I write out my prayers." Smiling she said, "Yes, I know, and you better listen to what I'm telling you."

Cavanaugh had its challenges but it remains an appointment near to my heart. While I was there, a parishioner named Danny decided that it was time to get the men's baseball dart team meeting again. We competed against other church teams and the standings of the baseball church league were printed on the sports page of the *Southwest Times Record*. I would love to be able to tell you that we won our division but, the reality is, every year, we were presented the Sportsmen of the Year Award which traditionally went to the cellar team. Some team members grumbled that our woes were due to the rabbi (which is what they called me) always throwing for and rarely ever hitting a homerun.

It was at Cavanaugh, due to the patience of that wonderful congregation, that I learned how to be a Methodist preacher. It was at Cavanaugh that I learned just how resilient small churches can be when so many cards are stacked against them, i.e. location, competition, and limited resources. It was at Cavanaugh that Rhonda and I traveled that relationship road from dating to engagement to marriage.

It was also at Cavanaugh that I began to get a glimpse into Methodism's troubled future. When I first went to the church (though I had read Bishop Wilke's book *And Are We Yet Alive?*) I didn't give much thought to the changes in culture and how that would affect mainline churches. Two years prior to my arrival at Cavanaugh, *Newsweek* had already featured an article, "From 'Mainline' to Sideline" but that didn't register much. That should have been required reading in my classes at seminary, but it wasn't. Like Nero playing while Rome burned, we studied Calvin. When I entered into the North Arkansas Conference, I thought it was like Rome and would last for centuries. Clearly my undergraduate major wasn't sociology.

It was at Cavanaugh that I began to examine Wilke's criteria for *Five Star Churches*. When I first read it, I thought it short-sighted and wondered if it like so many social-policy reforms would lead to unintended consequences. In my home church, St. Scholastica's, I don't remember attendance ever being kept, but I'm sure it was. Now that I had entered into the strange Protestant world where some churches placed worship attendance and last week's offering on a wooden board near the front of the church, the odd Protestant world where churches and clergy were given awards at annual conference for church-growth, I thought, "Well mercy, if that is the only criteria, give me enough latitude and I could grow a church. I imagine the temples on top of the mountain in Corinth had no trouble attracting attendees."

Churches were not measured for how many martyrs your congregation produced in the last year but by how much your worship attendance, Sunday School attendance, and other numerical criteria increased. Though I had deep loyalty and admiration for Wilke, I thought his *Five Star Churches* program a mistake. It also needs to be said that though I thought it misguided and wrongheaded, I admired Wilke for attempting to address an institutional crisis of unbelievable proportions.

Wilke wrote that "Wesley argued that growth was a sign of God's grace, decline a sign of decrease in grace."[4] The obvious and painful question for the clergy person to internalize is, what happens when growth doesn't occur? What happens when the congregation is reluctant to embrace the pastor due to race, gender, cultural issues, or other prejudices which can be as basic as, "This preacher isn't like the last preacher whom we loved and idolized? Get us another preacher like that one." When growth doesn't happen in a system that prioritizes growth above all else, then does that mean the clergy person no longer stands within the grace of God or at the very least, does it mean that the grace that he or she inhabits is decreasing?

The church-growth criterion can lead to an increase of clergy self-loathing for those whose zip codes are unfavorable, for those who faithfully serve congregations with hundred- year-old DNA and an over-abundance of silos. Clearly anyone could plainly see that hidden within the *Five Star Churches* programs is the fostering of unhealthy clergy competition, undue clergy stress, and long-term rising health premiums. And of course, clergy promotions, salary increases, in a system which prioritizes growth, go to those who produce results. This word of caution is not intended to suggest that numbers are not important as each number represents a child of God.

It is also problematic for the clergy whose churches have experienced tremendous growth as they are lionized by the system as gurus of growth that other clergy need to emulate. Gurus of growth are tempted to receive their positive affirmation from external results, which can foster the tendency to frenzied activity and not the hard work of inward spiritual growth. Furthermore, it was a system that rewarded appearance over substance.

The cultural storm was bigger than the clergy and was not and is not going to be solved through simple motivational speeches and trophies. From 1968 to 1988, the United Methodist Church lost two million members in the United States. (Since I have been serving full-time, another two million have gone missing.) Regardless of one's ideology, this cultural tsunami is not simply the result of ineffectual clergy. The inherent problem of that position is it assumes that the clergy were all that effective prior to the decline. The obvious and painful reality is that the culture of the country supported the work of the church. The storm that has been battering the church is made up of many components: the abolishment of the blue-laws, a rise in a consumer culture and an entertainment culture, the decline of positive regard for the church and clergy in the wider culture, an endless

4. Wilke, *And Are We Yet Alive?*, 15.

succession of clergy sex and malfeasance scandals, a rise in secularism, the decline of rural America and an increase in urban and suburban America, the Wal-Mart-ization of the church (meaning the rise of the megachurch and how that reflects cultural priorities of consumerism), declining birthrates, sociological trends of declining civic and community organizations, i.e. "bowling alone," and conflict in churches over worship, social ideologies, and ownership of property. Another component of Methodist decline, whose roots are found long before the United Methodist Church was founded, that needs further consideration is how, as it demanded more education from its clergy with the Master of Divinity becoming the standard degree for ministerial preparation and as many of its members increased economically, it no longer presented a compelling message to the poor and lower-classes. Historically, the Pentecostals stepped into the vacuum the Methodists left.

The hierarchy, so desperate to turn around a declining institution, lifted up in the wilderness not a symbol, model (church-growth) that would bring healing, but widespread sickness. The hierarchy, so desperate to turn around a crumbling institution, perhaps unintentionally or not, laid the blame too often as pilot error and the pilots were not church bureaucrats, but all those local church pastors who need to be motivated. As if the claim of Christ upon their lives, apparently, was not enough.

After two years in the church, I missed that which I had always taken for granted, studying theology, and decided to pursue a Master of Theology degree at Duke University with the thoughts of applying to a PhD program afterwards. It was difficult for me to leave Fort Smith, though Rhonda, a Carolina girl, was happy to be moving close to home. About a month before we left, the church having raised sufficient funds for the down payment purchased a home in the Colony South area for the new young preacher and his wife to move into.

III. EAST BOUND I–40, DESTINATION TOBACCO ROAD

After loading up the U Haul truck, we headed out east bound on I–40. Spending the night at Rhonda's grandparents in Alexander, which is located on the French Broad River outside of Asheville, we embarked the next day for Durham. I had gotten a job as one of the two Lock-Out personnel on Central Campus. Our responsibilities included during off hours (anytime other than 8 am to 5 pm Monday through Friday when the Central Campus

Housing Office was open) letting in undergraduates at one, two, or three in the morning, or some other god-awful hour, who had either lost their keys or were too intoxicated to remember that they were hanging from their back pockets. Our other glorious responsibility included plunging toilets. Later when I would interview for an associate pastor's job, one member of the Staff Parish Relations Committee (SPRC) asked me how my Central Campus duties prepared me for the work in the church and I answered, "The good aspect of Central Campus work is that you can see it before you step in it, unlike the parish."

Our apartment was on the second floor which was great except that mom, once I had moved to Fort Smith, insisted that I come and get my piano for she wanted to put an antique in the place the piano occupied. So, it too went with us to Durham. Carrying the piano up the flight of stairs was taxing and embarrassing as passing by students made comments. One night, while letting Christian Laettner into his apartment, I happily learned that he too had a piano.

It was great to be back on a university campus. Rhonda got a job as a nurse working in the Cardiothoracic Intensive Care Unit at Duke Hospital. We spent our free time taking in concerts, the arts, or just walking all around the campus: East Campus, the Duke Gardens, and basking in the gothic wonderland of West Campus. We visited various churches and settled on Trinity UMC. Because we were on Lock-Out Duty every other weekend, we watched campus TV worshipping with Duke Chapel. It was awe inspiring to listen to Will Willimon, the University Chaplain, and I marveled at how effective he was at communication. "No doubt," I thought, "that he was raised in the Methodist Church; it all comes so easy for him." I never will forget when Peter Gomes, Harvard's University Chaplain, began his sermon by saying, "How wonderful it is to be back preaching in St. Nicotine's."

I started work at Central Campus the first week in July and school did not begin until mid-August. Originally planning to do my work in nineteenth century continental theology but, after being at Duke for three weeks or so, I found myself contemplating something I never thought possible: I missed the local congregation. I missed the rhythms of community life: worship, fellowship, small-group studies and, of course, the Baseball Dart-Team. This was as big of a surprise to me as any in my life. What I did next was equally stunning. I changed the concentration of my degree from theology to pastoral theology. I did my work in pastoral theology with

Paul Mickey who had studied with Seward Hiltner who many consider to be the founding father of the discipline of pastoral psychology. For my minor in theology, I took classes from the liberationist theologian, Frederick Herzog, who had been a student assistant to Karl Barth in Basel. Herzog, a theologian's theologian, knew the developments of nineteenth and twentieth centuries European and American theology like the back of his hand. I imagine in his sleep he quoted *The Church Dogmatics* in German.

While at Duke, I did something that I had never done before. I actually read all the assignments, never missed a class unless I was sick, and worked on the papers prior to the 24-hour period in which they were due. This conversion had nothing to do with my religious beliefs and everything to do with the realization that since I was now married, I was no longer responsible for just myself. My actions affected another. But if the truth be told, though the grades improved, I missed the old way of being, yearning for spontaneity and freedom. I missed the lightness of being.

I chose pastoral psychology as I thought it would be most helpful when I returned to parish work. It turned out to be helpful not just to my skillset for vocational work, but it greatly enriched me personally as I started to examine all the ghosts which had haunted me from my childhood: my father's pre-mature death, his self-sabotaging behaviors, his addictions to alcohol, tobacco, and food. I never picked up the alcohol or tobacco addictions but the food dragon has slain me all my life. I reflected on my family of origins and pronounced behaviors within it: co-dependency and control issues that were let loose like the wild buffalos roaming the plains. Also, I spent time unpacking mom's role in it all, and reflecting on how my search for an idealized heavenly Father was a counter to the very broken vessel of clay that was my own father. It was at Duke that it began to settle down around me that I wouldn't ever totally be free from it, but that the greatest liberation was going to be like Eugene Peterson observed, "a long obedience in the same direction."[5]

In January, I notified the North Arkansas Conference that I decided against applying for PhD work and wanted to return to the parish in June. After a week or two, I got the phone call telling me that the person who

---

5. Eugene Peterson (1932–2018), the founding pastor of Christ Our King Presbyterian Church, served the congregation for twenty-nine years before he became a professor of spiritual theology at Regent College in Vancouver. He then retired to his home state of Montana. He was well-known not only for his spiritual writings, but also for his popular translation of the Scriptures (*The Message*). The rock group U2, ardent fans of Peterson's translation, promoted *The Message* on their website.

had been appointed to Cavanaugh decided that he too wanted to return to school and that I was being reappointed to Cavanaugh. I was delighted. In February, I called the District Superintendent and told him that we were unexpectedly expecting our first child and I asked, "Would we be covered by the Conference's insurance since this would be classified as a preexisting condition?" He gave me the number for the Conference Insurance person. I called her, and she said, "No problem. It will all be taken care of."

It was exciting to be at Duke that spring. For years, the sportswriters roasted the basketball team as always the bridesmaid but never the bride. Some called Coach K, Coach Choke, and sports analysts speculated on why Duke could never win the prize. Basketball fever took over the university as Duke progressed from one bracket to another until finally they made it to the Final Four. I'm sure the Duke vs. UNLV game took collective years off the student body's life expectancy, and the campus erupted when Duke defeated Kansas for the National Championship.

Early May, I had several movers coming to give estimates of what it would cost to move back to Fort Smith when the phone rang. It was the Benefits Officer for the Conference and she said, "Mike, we're not sure that you're covered." Immediately, my mind went to my nephew James' complicated delivery, extended time in the hospital, and mountainous medical bills. I asked, "Why not?" "Well last year we went with the General Board for Insurance. Used to be we could cover anything we wanted to but now we're not exactly sure if preexisting conditions are covered or not. Here's the number for the General Board, you call them and find out." I took down the number and called. Spoke with someone who said, "Well, we're pretty sure you'd be covered." I asked him to put in down in writing and send it to me. He never did. I called the DS. He didn't get it sorted out. Finally, frustrated with the bureaucracy, I called my DS and told him that we had 100 percent coverage at Duke, a free place to live, and we're not risking it. He said, "But you have to come back. You're already appointed." I said, "No, I don't."

Rhonda and I got busy with all the preparations for the birth of our first child: Lamaze classes, purchasing a crib and all the other things you need. I never knew one needed so many things. It was a glorious time and a fearful time. On September 25, our first child Laura came into the world at Duke University Hospital. The very night she was born, I went back to the apartment to meet some of Rhonda's family when the phone rang. It was a Senior Pastor of a church in Charlotte who said that he had got my name from so and so and that he was looking for an associate pastor. He asked if

I wanted to come and interview for the job. I exclaimed, "I just had a baby. I can't talk right now. Can I call you tomorrow?"

Upon returning to the hospital, I told Rhonda, "Some senior pastor from a church named Providence in Charlotte just called me up and asked me if I wanted to interview for a job." She said, "Don't tease me. That's not funny." I said, "No, it's true." She started to cry. If I didn't know better, I'd think she had doubts about me being the primary care-giver of our daughter while she continued to work at Duke until the next appointment year began in July. She strongly encouraged me to call him back the next day. I did. We talked for a while and the next week we met half-way in Thomasville at a chain restaurant of one kind or another. I believe a week after that, I was interviewing with the SPRC. They offered me a job and asked when I could begin. I said, "The first of November."

It was sad to leave Duke, a place of such beauty and a place where on any given day you could find a poet, writer, or academic signing books in *The Gothic Bookshop*. I stood in line, with my books, waiting to meet Reynolds Price and to get his autograph. I remembered how a former professor had told me that on a ship crossing the Atlantic a friend of Price's had lent him the typewritten pages of *A Long and Happy Life* before it was published.

Duke invited the Poet Laureate Joseph Brodsky to campus for a lecture. There he stood outside of the Brian Center surrounded by poets which included Mark Strand. Making my way with a copy of *To Urania*, I extended it to the great Russian-American poet asking him if he would be kind enough to sign it. He said, "Of course," and signed it with a smile: "Joseph Brodsky, Oct. 12, 1991, Chapel Hill." Closing the book, he handed it back to me. Thanking him, I walked away with my prize only to open it later, leaving me to wonder, had he been on so many different university campuses that they all started to look alike so much so that the great Nobel Prize winning poet did not even know which university campus he was on, or was it a dagger into my heart bursting Duke pomposity?

IV. Churches of Excellence

In November of 1991, I began serving as the associate pastor at Providence United Methodist Church. My responsibilities were various but specific charges included new member recruitment and membership nurture. Back in those days, recruiting new members to a suburban church like Providence in a southern city like Charlotte, which still operated somewhat as if

Christendom still existed, was not that difficult. The church, at that time, had an outstanding youth ministry, a good children's ministry, an excellent music program, and solid preaching from the pulpit. It wasn't like the 1950's where all you had to do was open the doors of the church and people flooded in, yet the church attracted people to it due to its ministries and worship. All I had to do, like the fisherman in a boat in the midst of a school of jumping fish was just hold out the net. Not all churches were like Providence back then but, even then, for churches like Providence, the times they were a changing and changing fast.

Sometime before I entered the Conference, it launched *Vision 2000*, a program focused on church growth. It didn't take long to learn the stars of the conference. They were the ones serving suburban churches located in the midst of new housing developments whose churches were growing in worship attendance at a fabulous rate. *Vision 2000* imported its model from Bishop Wilke, but instead of giving out *Five Star-Churches* plaques, the award given was *Churches of Excellence*. Excellence was measured by numerical increases.

This was the age where news reports of megachurches like Willow Creek in Barrington, IL, made it onto the pages of *The Charlotte Observer*. This was the age of the pink palace being built in south Charlotte sure that like *Field of Dreams* if you build it the masses will flock to it. This was the gilded ecclesiastical age where many in the institutional American church seemed to go after the church growth movement's mantra that bigger is better. Pastors measured each other's steeples. Contemporary worship music was all the rage, and pastors did their best to look hip. You never would find polyester in the crowd: all denim and tweed jackets for winter and seersucker for summer. Those pastors whose congregations demonstrated dynamic growth were given leadership positions within the conference. Everyone it seemed drank the Kool-Aid including me.

For systems under duress, often times, results become the idols of the moment. Not enough time was spent analyzing why a particular congregation in a particular social-matrix experienced growth or for asking questions like: Was the surrounding community exploding with new housing developments? Were the surrounding congregations embroiled in conflict? Was the marriage between pastor and congregation working for reasons that are less than desirable? Did the preacher give the congregation what they wanted, a watered-down, culturally-accommodated Gospel which presented Jesus as their therapist and self-improvement coach? Did the pastor present a Jesus that challenged the corrupt social order or was Jesus a chaplain who blessed the powers and principalities? The questions I heard more often than any other revolved around marketing, demographic studies, and facilities.

The most prestigious award given each year by our conference, at that time, was the Denman Award for Evangelism. Isn't it telling that we didn't have an annual conference award called the Kenosis Award given to the person who most represents emptying of oneself out in service to Christ? Traditionally the Denman Award went to those cool and smooth pastors of suburban churches surrounded by housing developments and exploding zip codes.[6] But as time wore on, I started to notice that all that glitters isn't gold. As time wore on, I started to read Eugene Peterson in an attempt to curb the effects of church growth on my soul.[7] But that was later and before that I drank more than a few glasses of that strange brew; some might say more than a case or two. As the years passed, I noticed that some of the Denman Award winners sacrificed way too much of themselves on the altar of numerical growth. Years would go by before the casualty reports trickled in: divorces, addictions, and other self-destructive behaviors. Years would go by before the church growth body count became apparent.

Though I loved Providence and Charlotte, I did not want to be a career associate. Desiring to be the captain of my own ship, after three appointment years, I requested a move. Having been affected by the conference values, I asked the DS for a suburban congregation, surrounded by a rapidly growing zip code. I never will forget when I went to meet him in his office. He said, "Boy do we have a great church for you. Mike, it is an absolutely wonderful congregation, Bethany UMC, full of lots of opportunity. It is located in West Jefferson; well actually, it is in a suburb of West Jefferson, Baldwin." I, not knowing North Carolina, experienced a racing heart at the mention of the word suburban. I thought this will be great. They will have a Harris Teeter and perhaps even a Borders Books and Music. I asked him where West Jefferson is located and he told me that it is about two hours north of Charlotte. He then shared my salary package, and all the church

6. I'm referencing a specific time period in WNCC's Conference life. There have been attempts since then to bring greater diversity to what represents the work of evangelism other than just numerical increases.

7. Another spiritual writer who was also of great help during this time was Henri Nouwen. Nouwen (1932–1996) a Roman Catholic priest from Holland served as a professor of practical theology at Notre Dame, Yale, and Harvard universities. His work *The Wounded Healer* became a standard text for the training of clergy.

numbers, i.e. worship attendance, Sunday school, etc. In closing he said, "Mike, the church has great, great potential."

The time came for us to meet with the leadership of our new appointment so we loaded up our car and Rhonda, Laura, and John and I traveled to the mountains. (John was born three months prior in Presbyterian Hospital in Charlotte.) We drove north on I-77 until we turned onto Highway 421 and took that until we got to Highway 221. As we drove, we saw lots of trees, but no Harris Teeters. We continued our ascent and, as we passed Fleetwood, my spirits were no longer sinking. They hit rock bottom. This suburbia had more cows than people. Rhonda said, "Oh honey, it will be great." I said something like, "Oh my Lord."

We pulled into the church and met the leaders and, I have to admit, we had wonderful conversations. We then toured the parsonage. But if there had been a door number two or three, I would have exited at that point. But there wasn't, and I'm grateful for Bethany is where I needed to be.

V. The Lost Colony and Mexico

While still in Charlotte, I called around to speak to ministers who had served in Ashe County to find out what it is like. One said, "When you get to the border, stop, get your cash exchanged, and your passport stamped, because you are entering a foreign land." Another said, "Mike they are a peculiar people. If they like you, they will go to hell for you and if they don't, you'll swear you're living there." As June came to an end, we loaded up our stuff in a U-Haul truck and headed north. The first forty days it rained almost every day. Not only was there not a Harris Teeter in Ashe County but also no Borders or even at that time a Wal-Mart or a Wendy's. We had indeed entered a new world, a world where relationships were more important than church growth, a world where mission was more important than marketing, a world where vegetables magically appeared on one's porch, and a world where life-long friendships were formed. Rhonda fell in love with Ashe County first, and I followed along. Even as I write this, all these years later, if my plan weren't to return some day to the family farm in Arkansas, it would be to buy a home in Ashe County. It was also during our time at Bethany that our third child, Emily, came into the world at Watauga Hospital in Boone.

I don't want you to think that Bethany was a perfect church. The perfect church doesn't exist, and the perfect pastor is an even greater illusion.

Bethany had its problems just like every church does, but it was a wonderful place to serve. In the middle of my fourth year at Bethany, missing theological conversations, I enrolled in a Doctor of Ministry program (DMin) at a school in the northeast. I already had started reading the books for the first course. Everything was set and that's where I would have matriculated if the next story that I'm about to relate didn't happen.

Scheduled to go on a mission trip to Mexico with the Wesley Foundation at Appalachian State University and wanting to be in good shape so I could keep up with those college students, I went out for a walk. I did what doctors tell you to do all the time, exercise. It was the 19th day in February (1998), a beautiful winter's day in Ashe County. Snow and ice still covered the ground, but I was a mountaineer at heart and gave no second thought to such conditions. I went over to Mountain Aire and met Mark, a friend and parishioner, and we set off for our normal trek around the golf course. But this day, instead of staying on the streets, we hiked across the golf course to check how the ice had damaged the greens. Mark, being the owner of the golf course, worried about them. We had a great walk and were almost done, when I descended down a small ditch. My feet gave way and if I had just stayed on the ground I would have been ok. But no, I had to jump back up, wanting to appear athletic, and I can truly attest that pride does come before the fall, and that's when I heard a sound I had never heard before.

As I lay on the frozen ground of Mountain Aire with my left foot lying flush to the soil in a way that I had never seen my left foot do before, as I lay staring at the cloudy gray February skies, my first thought was, "What happened to my guardian angel?" Growing up, the nuns told me about my guardian angel, even giving me holy cards with his picture on the front, sword in hand, and foot stomping down on some underworld miserable creature and on the back was a prayer of protection. Did he go out for coffee? There was no Starbucks in Ashe County at that time and thus I'm sure he had a long trip. My second thought came a little bit later. I began reflecting on the Scripture passage, Psalm 35:15, "But at my stumbling they gathered in glee."

The reason why I thought of this Scripture is that when the ambulance guys arrived, they looked down at me and then over to Mark and a couple of his golf course employees who had assembled, and they said, "Boy now, he's a big one. We'll need you all's help in lifting him up." I thought, "Everybody's a critic. What do you guys work for Weight Watchers or something?" And when I got to the hospital there's something about pain and tragedy that makes compete strangers comfortable and brazen. As you're being wheeled down the halls, people who you are just passing by, who you've never even seen before ask, "Wow, how'd you do that?" When you relay, "Well I was out walking and slipped," they look down at you lying on the gurney like you're a complete moron. I mean it's okay if you wreck your motorcycle and break your leg. Or it's okay if you're flying a plane over Africa and it crashes. Or if you're running with the bulls in Spain and trip and one of those monsters' step on your leg, well that's okay. That's the stuff of legends, a true Heminwayesque way of going, but out one day walking, how humiliating.

Let me tell you, it's humiliating when your spouse, while you're in the room as if you're the village idiot, asks, "Well doctor, how's his bone density?" As if I wouldn't know what she's talking about. Trust me, I heard the jokes. The first Sunday I was gone from the pulpit, the chair of the Administrative Council told the congregation, "Our preacher is not here today because he fell from grace, but due to a lack of grace he fell."

Rhonda declared that I was not a good patient, and some nurses were timid about entering my room. I was also, I imagine, not a joy to live with when I got home. My patience with being broken was limited. The first week while lying in bed, I would dose off and relive the nightmare of falling only to awaken startled, jumping, and have pain shoot though my leg. The church couldn't have been more caring, bringing meals. During this duration of illness, I began to reexamine the DMin program in which I had enrolled. In a strange way, it was somewhat like a Schelling re-do and I felt I needed more practical skills. A friend was doing his doctorate at Southern Methodist University in Evangelism. I had long had an interest in evangelism, in sharing the good news of the Gospel in hopes that it would liberate others as it had liberated and continues to liberate me.[8] By this time, having already read through Eugene Peterson's trilogy on ministry, I wanted to know how to do authentic evangelism without sacrificing it on the idol of church growth. Just because some engage in evangelistic malpractice is no excuse for the church to not take evangelism with utmost conviction, determination, and prayerful expectation.

---

8. One of the most painful realizations of the want-to-be evangelist is that what is most liberating to you will not be necessarily empowering to your closest friends and family members. Just because Christianity is precious to you does not mean that by osmosis those nearest to you will also hold it close. C.S. Lewis also found this to be true. See *The Oxbridge Evangelist*, 202.

VI. Galloping Mustangs

Southern Methodist University's Doctor of Ministry program provides its students with a model of a reflective practitioner, a model I immediately took to heart. It was in a course for William J. Abraham that I first read his book *The Logic of Evangelism*. Abraham, a Northern Irishman, studied with Basil Mitchell at Oxford University. Mitchell took over the leadership of the Socratic Club at Oxford once C.S. Lewis resigned his presidency. *The Logic of Evangelism* was a book that clicked, like tumblers on the lock that all fell into place. In the work, Abraham defined evangelism as "primary initiation into the Kingdom of God."[9] Evangelism encompasses such works as proclamation, catechesis, prayer, baptism, and confirmation.[10]

Abraham critiqued the Church Growth Movement noting the tension between authentic evangelism and the principles of church growth, which is beholden to a "fierce pragmatism."[11] Abraham, in a work published in 1989, took note of the desperation of the mainline churches to reverse their steep decline and observed how they were ready to make use of any magical concoction to change the course of decline and save the institutional church. He spoke a word of caution to the clergy: "Thus there develops a new canon of saints and heroes whose primary credentials are their ability to produce external results."[12]

The Church Growth Movement presented an institutionalized spiritual temptation that sadly too many in the denomination of decline failed. It is also a temptation that I have succumbed to, time and again. As part of a six-person design team for a leadership development program for clergy in my conference, what we looked at, over and over again, as models of fruitful ministry were megachurches which were, for the most part, new church plants that grew exponentially under a charismatic leader and a well-executed team. But what I couldn't escape feeling after departing from each of the megachurches we visited was that what was being lifted up was not the host, not the body of Christ, but the personality of the Senior Pastor. The church-growth model often works well in new church starts where one can create a worship-style that resonates with the surrounding community and market the church addressing the community's personality,

9. Abraham, *The Logic of Evangelism*, 13.

10. Abraham, 104.

11. Abraham, 77.

12. Abraham, 78.

socio-economic values, and needs. The great difficulty with lifting up the church-growth model up as the standard is that 99 percent of churches are not recent new church starts. The pastors of these established churches with their own long-standing worship styles and traditions are sent off to be trained at the church of the moment only to return to churches and then attempt to bring change. I have referenced the damage that chasing this agenda has done to the clergy, but it has also exacted a cost to many parishioners.[13] Stanley Hauerwas, a lay Methodist and a theologian at Duke University, presented in vivid detail what is was like to be in a church where the preacher after having returned from the church-growth seminar began to make changes in order to facilitate a program of church-growth.[14]

Clergy who went off to conferences that educated them on how to grow a church often returned to congregations full of people who chose the church because they liked it as it was. Often times, in the midst of the conflict that ensued, clergy were tempted to label congregants who were resistant to loud praise music, descending screens, and an invasion of superficial good feeling, as the opposition, obstacles to the church's vibrant future. When Hauerwas objected to the changes that his pastor brought, she accused him of being against "evangelization."[15] He responded that he was not against evangelization but in opposition to employing "economic modes of life incompatible with the gospel."[16]

Again, problematic to running institutions is the tendency for "us vs. them" to emerge. As Thomas G. Long noted that many churches were engaged in the "worship wars."[17] In these painful clashes, generational conflicts played out with incredible amounts of pressure put upon the oldest generations as if they were/are the problems keeping the church from growing. Many of them felt indignant and not valued even though they are the ones often carrying the greatest part of the church's budget. Adding insult to injury, implicit promises are made that if the church makes the changes then young people will want to attend their church. Of course, the older generations are held hostage to the hope of the church's future against their love of the church in the present. They are held hostage to a hope that

13. Gehring, "A Difficult Obedience."

14. Hauerwas, *Hannah's Child*, 221, 258, 259.

15. Hauerwas, 259.

16. Hauerwas, 259.

17. Long is the Bandy Professor of Preaching Emeritus at Candler School of Theology, Emory University, and author of *Beyond the Worship Wars*.

the advocates for change cannot guaranty as the millennial generation continues to demonstrate little attraction to the institutional church. If in those well-marketed and packaged church growth seminars, more time was spent engaging critically with the sociological trends of the Great Ecclesiastical Tsunami, then some of the participants perhaps wouldn't be as prone to rush back to their churches like bulls let loose in a china shop.

Obviously, my sympathy is not only with the laity but also with the clergy; I too have broken quite a few dishes in the china shop. The clergy feel sandwiched between expectations projected onto them and expectations they themselves take on trying to rescue a denomination in crisis. No one can save the United Methodist Church but Jesus and, even for Him, it's going to take some time. Preachers become bone-weary watching the effects of the cultural storm batter against the institutions that they love. It is not easy to lead a church under the best of conditions, as the cliché of past years is accurate: "running a church is like herding cats." But in the midst of these turbulent conditions, as membership, worship attendance, and financial resources decline, it is even more exhausting.

Another challenge that United Methodist laity suffer from is theological whip-lash. This is also tied to Protestantism's Achilles heel. Having no catechism and no real mechanism for regulating the teaching and preaching offices of the church, the laity are left to endure an onslaught of clergy opinions and ideology that sometimes masquerade as truth statements. Not having a pope can leave a denomination open to the charge that every preacher, in fact, becomes a pope. When one Methodist pastor leaves and the new one arrives, there can be a dramatic continuum of theological positions represented. In one way, this is one of the strengths in Methodism, especially for us clergy, but for the laity, how confusing it would be if the former pastor had been preaching a cultural conservative, almost fundamentalist version of the faith steeped in inerrancy and intolerance, and the next one is a radical liberationist preaching a social-gospel infused with Marxist ideology. The poor parishioner struggles to makes sense of a language in which she or he may not have been properly schooled.

The DMin in evangelism was helpful in conceptually wrapping my mind around what constitutes and what does not constitute authentic evangelism. As my time grew near the end with graduation on the horizon, Abraham invited me to be a part of a new think-tank he was forming called The Polycarp Fellows. It would be lodged within the Center for Evangelism and Missional Church Studies at Perkins School of Theology (SMU) and would be comprised of pastors, missionaries, and theologians who would gather together, at least annually, to think through the current issues of evangelism and missiology. I quickly replied, "Count me in."

VII. United or Untied: Mainline Methodism at the Crossroads

Sitting at my desk as I write these lines, I look up at the ordination certificate on the wall signed by Bishop Wilke, down at the Canterbury tokens scattered on my desk, and over to a picture of Salvador Dali's *Last Supper* scotch-taped to the bookcase. What to make of it all? What to make of this impasse? For years, some failed to take stock of just how deeply divided the UMC church was/is, and assumed that, after a few more years, the church would catch up with the culture. But the storm that has overtaken us did not fall upon us unaware. For years, it hung as menacing clouds on the horizon. Before we turn our attention to the eye of the storm, allow me to share why Polycarp became for me like a refuge.

I've been attending Polycarp gatherings for over seventeen years. It has been a great help to be a part of long-term theological conversations, and I doubt that I would still be serving in the local church without Polycarp. It has renewed my soul, over and over again, and without it I would have surely ended up a burnt-out case.

Over those years, Polycarp's membership has fluctuated. Some who were in the beginning are still a part of it, and others have exited making room for new members. We read texts, present papers, and debate the issues affecting the church: racism, sexism, secularism, Islam's confrontation with the west, homosexuality, Pentecostalism, ecclesiology, missiology, evangelization, philosophy of religion, epistemology, and certainly other topics that I have forgotten. We represent a variety of opinions and perspectives ranging from progressive to conservative, from those whose ministry contexts are in the first-world to those in the third-world, from male to female, from the local church to university departments of theology, and physics.

The long-term conversations confirmed in me that to state that we are more polarized now than ever before is an overstatement. Humanity, inherently, has a tendency toward brokenness, polarization, fragmentation, exclusion, hostility, war, and getting oneself kicked out of paradise. East of Eden, we've long slain each other in word and deed. What is different now is just how convenient it is to do so, as accessible as one's finger tips through the use of Facebook, Twitter, and email. I remember back in the glory days of the eighties, the days of Springsteen and Reagan, that if some serious ideologue wanted to influence Methodist ministers, then he or she would have to type up their comments, run them off on a photocopier, stuff them into envelopes, address, stamp, and mail them. Now in a matter of a few seconds one can communicate on Twitter to millions.

As one formed by Roman Catholicism, I miss the days of having a Pope to settle doctrinal disputes. My Catholic clergy friends tell me that my idealism and my longing for the days long gone often bests me, and I fail to take account of just how messy the Roman Catholic Church remains even in the midst of having a Pope. Having a Pope has not spared them from fractious debates. Even though I know that, still there are days when I wax sentimental for a past that is gone; those supposed golden days when the institution possessed a mechanism for calming the storms. Nostalgia is a drug I regularly ingest.

The crisis of the United Methodist Church looms and the purpose of this work is not to wade into the debate weighing the merits or weaknesses of the acceptance or rejection of practicing homosexuals among clergy or of advocating or opposing ecclesiastical same-sex marriage. But any reader can see that due to my father's exclusion from the Eucharistic, and with Phil's experience of rejection and judgment by his own faith community, my prejudice is toward inclusion. Even with saying that, inclusion best not be turned into an idol; idols have a way of breaking people's hearts and lives apart.

The church, from its beginnings, has always had moral standards and each generation struggles with what they mean. Every generation determines the rules that will be strongly enforced and the ones that will receive a lighter touch. Every day, local congregations make decisions over whether their buildings will be gun-free zones or not, over who can work with children and youth and whether they will have to have criminal background checks or not. Every congregation decides who gets elected into leadership positions and whether the moral life of leaders is important to the community or not: is it okay if the treasurer embezzles the church's monies or is that problematic? Is it acceptable for the shepherd to sleep with the sheep? Is it tolerable if the paid staff of the church simply quit showing up for work but continue cashing their paychecks? Standards have always been a part of community life and will continue to be.

The difficulty for the United Methodist Church is, as any commentator will tell you, that if the solution to our conflicted state were simple then we would have solved it long ago. The church has been arguing about homosexuality since at least 1972, and the denomination was founded in 1968. It is of little wonder that a reconciling position that would please everyone has not been attained when one considers the theological space that each side has staked out. The conservatives feel that if they sanction same-sex marriage and give into the tremendous pressure placed upon them from both the culture and the progressive wing of the church then they would, in effect, deny Jesus as the authoritative standard. Often in arguing this position Matthew 19:5 is quoted; Jesus said, "For this reason a man shall leave his father and mother and be joined to his wife, and the two shall become one flesh." (NRSV) Those who ask the conservatives to capitulate to same-sex marriage are, in effect, asking them to abandon Jesus as their theological bedrock.

The progressive position is also well-defined: Jesus' very nature is one of radical love and he would not wish to see walls that divide; he would not practice exclusion. Those who ask the progressives to capitulate are, in effect, asking them to deny their theological bedrock of Jesus as the author, architect, of radical inclusion, hospitality, and love. Obviously, the previous characterizations are cursory, at best, and there are many resources available for both positions that are scholarly and well-argued.[18] It is not my intention, as already mentioned, to advocate for one side or the other. The reader can make up one's own mind. But what I draw attention to, in the portraits presented, is that both sides are trying to live faithfully into what they believe Jesus demands.

The United Methodist Church is a little late arriving at the crossroads of implementing change to its positions of marriage and ordination. The Presbyterian Church (USA) has already passed through the intersection and lost a significant number of churches and parishioners due to its embrace of same-sex marriages and the ordination of practicing homosexuals. The Evangelical Lutheran Church and the Episcopal Church, likewise, have already confronted these issues and though they are on the other side, they too have lost a significant number of members and churches. They are quickly becoming shadows of who they once were. One church-growth

18. The literature is plentiful; a few examples are: Gagnon, *The Bible and Homosexual Practice*, Achtemeier, *The Bible's Yes to Same-Sex Marriage*, and Gagnon and Via, *Homosexuality and the Bible*.

specialist speculated that Mainline Churches, if they don't reverse the trend, have only have 23 Easters left to go.[19] I don't know if he marked it that way knowing that it only took one Easter to turn it all around and that light breaks at dawn or if he intended it be more like a drinking-song: "23 Easters to go, 23 Easters to go, mark one off, look now it's gone, 22 Easters to go."

At the last General Conference of the United Methodist Church, the delegates decided not to keep kicking the can down the road but to have a special called General Conference to deal explicitly with the issue of homosexuality.[20] A special commission was established charged with making specific recommendations to the church that would hopefully provide a way forward. The Western Jurisdiction, feeling that the church had waited long enough, elected the Reverend Karen Oliveto as the first openly lesbian United Methodist bishop. Obviously, the conservative side of the church felt that the good faith that they had put in the Way Forward was betrayed by the delegates of the Western Jurisdiction. The liberals felt euphoric that their deep resistance would bring about change, and those who inhabit the middle were painfully aware that the impending change could just as easily end in schism. In the eyes of some, what had been a deeply polarized situation became an institution fractured almost beyond repair.

Regardless of however the United Methodist Church solves its dilemma over sexuality, whether it remains united with some kind of internal accommodation or whether it splits into two or three denominations, it will not then enter into a denominational magical state of peace. No Garden of Eden is around the corner. Protestantism began with a protest. Division is in its DNA.[21] When one issue is resolved another one will surface. Methodists have fought over alcohol, tobacco, and slavery, whether to have bishops or not, desegregation, worship styles, justice, gender, and race issues.

When it became emotionally real to me that United Methodism really could fracture, I was troubled. Truthfully, I thought, "Are you kidding me? I joined a Tower of Babel denomination that's going to crumble in upon itself?" Like many, I've lifted up unity almost as an idol. But the unity we speak of is more of an illusion. The old clergy joke, which is nowhere

19. Stetzer, "If it doesn't stem its decline, Mainline Protestantism has just 23 Easters left."

20. May 2016, Portland, Oregon.

21. Division also seems to be multiplying. In 1800, it was estimated that 500 Christian denominations existed; now, there are more than 43,000. "Century Disunity," 8.

as funny as it once was, is that the United Methodist Church is not tied together by theology or practice but by the property clause and the pension fund. The question that the constant wars made manifest is, how do we treat people who hold positions that conflict with our own? One would hope that we, the body of Christ, would view others as sacred vessels of God's Holy Spirit and not degenerate into mean-spiritedness, name-calling, and gossip. But sadly, in this long and protracted struggle, that has not been the case and damage has been done. Accusations hurled. Sins committed. As I write this, we are a long, long ways from Ash Wednesday, but we, as a church and as individuals, need to get there as quick as we can.

I wonder about the long-term spiritual damage that has been inflicted on the United Methodist Church, and I worry sometimes if the only reason why we are staying together is that it is simpler than a lengthy legal battle over the tremendous assets of the denomination. There are times when it appears that both extremes have very little charity left toward the other. It's difficult for the denomination to embody the love of God when members are slugging each other with verbal sledge-hammers. I've heard conservatives described as bigots, gay-haters, theological-Neanderthals, Holy Spirit-stiflers, and Pharisees by which the opponents mean legalistic and hard-hearted. If you think of it that is not a caricature that Joseph of Arimathea, Nicodemus, or Gamaliel would have appreciated. The progressives have been called apostates, theological light-weights, so open-minded that their brains fall out, leftists, and haters of the authority and discipline of the United Methodist Church. It's time for the swords to be beaten into ploughshares; it's time for the war of words to give way to the Gospel of grace and truth, recognizing the deep impasse and finding charity for theological opponents.

The early church father, Tertullian, said that the Roman pagan critics marveled at how much the Christians love each other. Perhaps, people are saying that about the United Methodists in some part of the universe, but I haven't heard it. What I have heard people wonder about is: "What's wrong with the Methodists?" "Aren't they supposed to have a method?" "The WWE appears positively utopian compared to the UMC's General Conference." (Well ok, the last one actually came from me.) Some want to minimize all this and say that all families squabble, and this is just a little disagreement that we're having. I would concur with that as long as the Hatfield-McCoy feud could also be labeled a small little family disagreement. I imagine a lot of Pagan and secular critics looking at Methodist dysfunction would say, "Enough already. Just get a divorce. It will be better for your children." Of course, the truth is it wasn't all rainbows, sunflowers, and unicorns in the early church. Paul and Barnabas split from each other because they couldn't solve their disagreement any other way. And a few hundred years later, some in the early church sought to solve their theological disagreements through the use of blunt force.

The reason why I no longer hold to unity as a golden calf is due to the casualty count of a denomination constantly fighting amongst itself: the wear, the worn-out souls, the battle-fatigue, and the palpable despair. Like the break of day, the realization dawned that a separate peace might be better than dehumanization. Mind you, I'm not advocating disunity. If we split over the issue of homosexuality or some other issue someday further down the road, I will not only grieve the loss of the current configuration of the United Methodist Church, but will consider such schism sinful. If the right pushes out the left, or if the left pushes out the right, we will no longer be people of the big tent that houses a wide spectrum of ideological positions. If we dissect, fracture, or fragment, I will yearn for unity, but we live in a Christ-haunted world riddled with sin. What is clear, if the denomination divides, is that after the split, congregations will remain. Within the congregations, unity of opinion will not hold. Congregations will mirror the diversity of opinions contested in the denomination but since they are used to living together holding quite a wide spectrum of political, economic, and social opinions, they will find a way onward. If it comes down to a vote, they will lose members from one end of the continuum to the other, but a remnant will remain. Congregations will pick up the pieces seeking to be participants in the kingdom of God as it is expressed both in the local church and beyond.

If the rupture occurs, Methodist churches will still gather to proclaim the Gospel, to break the bread, and to share the cup. In all of our dividedness, we will still pray for unity. In all our jaggedness, we will name our sins. Our churches will gather for communion and as broken sinners riddled with contradictions we will come forward and partake of the body and blood of Christ. We will come forward with our tattoos, with our bellies over our belt buckles, with our worries about our children, grandchildren, parents, troubled marriages, substance abuse, with fears about the cost of college, nursing homes, and home-foreclosures. We will come forward with all of our fragmented, disappointing political, social, and denominational ideologies and consider them all as dross compared to the life-giving sacraments that will sustains us until time itself fades into eternity. We will come forward in packed sanctuaries and in rooms with more seating opportunities than bodies. We will come forward desperate for the Other, for the transcendent, for that which reveals our hypocrisies and loves us anyway. We will come forward and partake.

Epilogue

I. Treasure Hunting

AFTER MOM'S DEATH, I had the unpleasant task of cleaning out her house. It's a work in progress really, and I've spent the last few vacations driving that seemingly never ending road of I–40 back home to continue the task. Mom was a hoarder, and there was so much stuff in her house that you could barely walk through it. Upon first glance one would want to shout, "Bring in a very small bulldozer." But you can't because in between old books that one would normally care nothing about are tucked away a family picture or a letter from some long lost relative. You have to sort through everything as you hunt for misplaced memories. One of the more amusing things was mom's massive record collection even though she didn't listen to records: puzzling really. In the midst of sorting through all of this, I didn't find the one record I was looking for.

When my brother and I were children, we used to listen to this old 33 rpm LP. You've got to remember this is back before the days of iPhones, iPods, Nintendo's, Play Stations, Cable TV, and Laptop computers. It is summertime, the fans are blowing, the windows are open, the light is draining from the sky, and the cicadas are singing their song. We're huddled around a boxed record player listening to the well-worn album as the narrator tells the story of *Treasure Island*.

Transported to another time, we listen to the story of Jim Hawkins, the son of innkeepers. In the Admiral Benbow Inn in southwest eighteenth century England, the story begins as a man in hiding, Billy Bones, who is a drunker old sailor, takes his lodging. After being visited by Black Dog, then Pew and, after receiving the black spot note, dies of a stroke. Jim and his mother look in Billy Bones' chest to get the money that they are due for his room and board. Upon hearing pirates coming down the hall, Jim's mom grasps only part of what they are owed, and he grabs an oilskin packet to compensate for the rest as they make their escape. Later when opening it, a treasure map is discovered and the journey is a foot.

It was from *Treasure Island* that I learned some valuable lessons; X marks the spot, don't trust pirates, and always be on the lookout for one legged sailors with parrots on their shoulders; important lessons to learn and retain. I wish I could say that they served me well, but I didn't realize back then that menacing pirates and hobbling sailors transporting parrots don't always look the part. Sometimes they come disguised as angels of light. What we learned at the end of 2007, as Wall Street decimated Main Street, is that sometimes pirates come wearing Armani suits.

When I was a teenager, I got into metal detecting and found Civil War bullets, rusty beer cans, a ton of corroded nails, and a few old coins. Regretfully I never found any of de Soto's missing gold. There is something alluring about being a treasure hunter; a sense of adventure and the wild world waiting to reveal hidden wealth. Of course, the treasures that one seeks to find are valuables that someone else hid away; they buried them with the hope that one day they could return and claim their prize. Only for one reason or another, life interrupted. Life interrupts all our carefully laid out or haphazardly designed and executed plans. But however it unfolds, we are left wondering about roads not traveled. Who would I have been if my parents never moved to Arkansas? Would I have become one of those who ride the zeitgeist on a surfboard? I don't know the answer to that. What I do know is the journey that I have traveled.

I went on a treasure hunt of sorts, a pilgrimage, wanting to find the perfect church home, a place where broken people were not excluded from the sacraments, a place where community exuded life and not stifled hope. I'm not alone in this as American Christianity has been greatly shaped by people jumping from one church to another hoping to find a place where they deeply resonate spiritually. Some people also jump from church to no involvement in organized religion. Some board the ship called None sailing into the relaxing waters of drinking Starbucks Coffee and reading *The New York Times* on Sunday morning instead of fighting the hustle and bustle of getting to church. Some jump off the boat of Christianity because somewhere along the way someone excluded them or a family member from God's grace. Some sail away leaving church divisions and ideological fights behind. People jump from church to church and others leave it for all kinds of reasons. One of the problems often made is to confuse the church as Institution for the Church Triumphant. It is a painful mistake to make. The United Methodist Church, the Assemblies of God, and the Roman Catholic Church are all human constructions no matter how much anyone wants to argue the opposite. Though God gave birth to the Church, the actual institutions, the legal entities are organized and run by humans who are fallen and make mistakes. Sometimes they try to protect the assets of the institution by sacrificing those who are most vulnerable. Sometimes it takes newspapers and lawyers to awaken the church from its self-satisfied slumber.

This is not to say that institutions don't have their place; they most certainly do. God can use institutions but regretfully sometimes institutions use God and people. Every denomination sins; they just sin differently, and Methodism is not perfect. It is far from the celestial city on earth, and the good Lord knows that Methodism has much to atone for but nevertheless it is one of my home churches. As I said in the beginning of this work, I'm like a man with two passports.

What Bill Lane taught me so many years ago is the inescapable conclusion that Christ calls us into community. The New Testament clearly records that Christ did not call us into a perfect community. The early church bears witness to just how messy, discordant, and sometimes unpleasant community can be. Yet nevertheless Christ calls us into relationship with one another. As the future proceeds into directions currently beyond our knowledge, we don't know how the great denominations will weather the changing cultural storms but what we do know is that God will have a church. The ecclesiastical landscape may be completely different. It may be much more influenced by house churches than by megachurches but whatever unfolds, the witness of the apostolic church is that the universal church is of God and the Spirit will blow wherever the Spirit chooses.